Spiritual Quest

also by the author from Paulist Press —

The Art of Christian Listening

Christian Foundations (with Kathleen Fischer)

Coming Down the Mountain

A Counselor's Prayer Book (with Kathleen Fischer)

Facing Discouragement (Kathleen Fischer)

The First Two Years of Marriage (with Kathleen Fischer)

Promises to Keep (with Kathleen Fischer)

SPIRITUAL QUEST

A Guide to the Changing Landscape

Thomas Hart

Paulist Press
New York/Mahwah, N.J.

Cover design by Nicholas T. Markell

Library of Congress Cataloging-in-Publication Data

Hart, Thomas N.
  Spiritual quest: a guide to the changing landscape / Thomas Hart.
    p. cm.
  Includes bibliographical references.
  ISBN 0-8091-3906-5 (alk. paper)
  1. Spiritual Life--Christianity. I. Title
  BV4501.2H3634 1999
  248.4--dc21

                                                    99-045388
                                                    CIP

Published by Paulist Press
997 Macarthur Boulevard
Mahwah, New Jersey 07430

www.paulistpress.com

Printed and bound in the
United States of America

TABLE OF CONTENTS

INTRODUCTION

You probably picked up this book because you too are a spiritual pilgrim. Your life is a mystery, even to you. Joined in various ways to others, yet ultimately alone, you make your way across the puzzling terrain of this world. Sometimes you wonder where you are going, or why you are even here. Often you muse on what you see going on around you.

Perhaps you were raised a Christian. As you became an adult, you had to decide what to do with that. You may always have loved and appreciated it, and just kept developing it as you went along. On the other hand, as you matured you may have found difficulties with it, felt you did not get much out of going to church and, as your life moved in new directions, just let it fade to the back roads of your mind.

Life keeps forcing questions upon you though. What is it all about anyway? What am I supposed to be and do? Where can I find some sense of direction? How do I fill the big empty space inside? What do I teach my children? And you begin thinking about spirituality.

As you look around, you notice that the spiritual landscape has changed. The mainline Christian churches have suffered a major decline in membership over the last thirty years. Yet there seems to be a new spiritual vitality in the air. New Age spirituality has attracted a broad following. Megachurches of an interdenominational sort have sprung up in the suburbs

1

and draw very well. There are major series on spirituality on public television: Joseph Campbell on myth, Huston Smith on world religions, the Genesis series on pivotal Bible stories. Books about God and spirituality make the best-seller lists. And though it is true that the mainline churches are losing members,[1] two branches of Christianity, quite different from the mainstream churches and also quite distinct from each other, are enjoying pronounced growth: fundamentalism, the most clear-cut and confident of the Christian approaches, and pentecostalism, the most experiential and emotive. This tells you that amid the confusion of so many spiritual and secular currents today, the *certainty* offered by fundamentalism, and the *live contact* with the Transcendent offered by pentecostalism, are assurances people hunger for.[2]

Those who are leaving the mainline churches are not doing it easily. You may have done it yourself. It is painful to leave the church of your childhood, of your parents, and your parents' parents. It has formed and nurtured you. It is hard to abandon a community, a liturgy, an entire tradition that has contributed so viscerally to who you are. You do so in the end only because again and again this church fails to meet your needs. Or you may still choose to stay. You still believe in your church, love it, and want it to change and grow. You are willing to put your shoulder to the plow to help your church become what it needs to be, patiently enduring its present shortcomings, still finding treasure at its core.

Whether you have left your church or stayed with it, if you are interested in the spiritual life this book is for you. It is a pilgrim's guide to a much changed and still evolving spiritual landscape. Whatever your religious status, you are probably asking yourself questions like these: How do I deepen and strengthen my spiritual life? How can I judge what is authentic and what spurious, what helpful and what fruitless or even harmful, among the ideas and practices I find around me? What church or other spiritual community shall I join? Shall I practice Buddhist meditation? Join a New Age group? Cultivate Native American spirituality? If I do, am I still a Christian? Does it make any difference? What do I really believe? On what can I confidently base my life?

I am a seeker myself, always have been. I know the experience from the inside and consider it one of the most enlivening activities of my whole life. I have long been in dialogue with others engaged in the spiritual quest. For thirty years or so, as a teacher of theology and spirituality, I have engaged the questions and concerns of Christian pilgrims. During the same years, I have served as spiritual guide to many on an individual basis. I am Roman Catholic, and professionally both a theologian and a therapist.

I delight in this new spiritual quest, with its wide-ranging appetite, its willingness to take risks and create some new synthesis, its seizing of the initiative and assumption of personal responsibility. I see it as a positive development in humankind's spiritual history. It may even represent a new stage of maturity. It seems to signal a paradigm shift occurring in our experience of the Transcendent, a change paralleling the shift taking place in the way we view the universe.

I welcome and am eager to consider all that is newly proposed. At the same time, I know the lasting value of the master story in relation to which my own life still finds its grounding and direction.[3] I would like to enrich the new spiritual quest with the wealth of insight and experience stored in the Christian tradition. At the same time, I would like to prod the established churches to a challenging but exhilarating resurrection.

My chief convictions are two:

1. There is so much that is valuable in the Christian spiritual tradition, now with some two thousand years of lived experience, that it would be a waste, at least for Christians, to throw it away and start all over.

2. But the tradition really needs renewal—a rethinking, an adaptation to new knowledge and needs, and a fresh presentation that will strike people today with a ring of relevance and of truth. Church structures need an overhaul too.

I will be calling attention to the perennial values in the tradition. And, with the help of many others who have done important theological work in the last several decades, I will set forth some of the reformulation of the tradition, solid and stimulating work with which the churches, by and large, have not caught up.[4] I especially want to present new ways of thinking about God, about Jesus, about sexuality, and about spirituality.

As I ruminated in the early going on the contours of this book, I realized I needed help. I needed a really clear sense of where people were in their spiritual quest, especially this hungry, present and former Christian population of whom I have been speaking. What exactly were they seeking, what were they sure of, and what questions were they pondering? Were they still going to church? Why or why not?

Some eighty persons, fifty-five women and twenty-five men, were kind enough to answer a questionnaire I developed.[5] They range in age from their twenties to their eighties. Sixty percent are of Roman Catholic origin; 40 percent of Protestant or Episcopal origin. About half are still going to church regularly, half not, though almost all of them once were regulars. To these people, who have guided my writing, I am most grateful. I realize that this small sample of the Christian population does not constitute a sufficient basis for scientific research. Yet these articulate respondents do provide a concrete sense of where many people raised in the Christian churches are today. Their remarks, sprinkled throughout these pages, give flesh and blood to the general ideas I present.

I open by sketching the contemporary worldview, the universe as we know it today. This may, at first blush, seem a bit remote from the spiritual quest. Yet it has unmistakable bearing on it. Our universe, as science depicts it for us, is ever the context of our spiritual probings. The way we know the cosmos has a lot to do with how we think about the Mystery. And so I will set forth the contemporary worldview, and then reflect on its implications for our understanding and experience of God.

Next, I will try to define that nebulous reality which has caught the popular imagination, spirituality, and see how it relates to religion. Then I will suggest criteria for discerning what is helpful and what is questionable where the spiritual life is concerned, both for individuals and for groups. Next, I will take a fresh look at Jesus to see what he might have to offer us as spiritual pilgrims. Then, in the light of his intimate relationship with the Mystery, I will explore our own religious experience and probe our possibilities for a relationship with the Mystery. Next, I will offer ten concrete principles for the undergirding of a healthy Christian spirituality. Then I will bring sexuality into the discussion, showing that there is an intrinsic link between our sexual and spiritual lives. Finally, I will catalogue the many movements both inside and outside organized religion that manifest a new spiritual vitality, and name the challenge and the opportunity they present to the churches.

You may want to explore more on your own some of the issues raised here. There are leads for your reading in the notes. At the end of each chapter, there are also questions and exercises for personal reflection, assimilation, and discussion.

You picked up this book, fellow seeker, because you too are on a spiritual journey. I hope you will find insight and perspective here, which will help you navigate your own passage. May these pages whet your appetite for the quest, lead you more deeply into the riches of a tradition that is mature yet ever capable of freshness, and make you a more discerning judge of other ideas and practices you might wish to incorporate into your spiritual life.

Chapter One

The New Cosmology and the Mystery

My religion consists of a humble admiration of
the illimitable superior spirit who reveals himself in the slight details we are able to perceive
with our frail and feeble mind.

—*Albert Einstein*

Time was, and it was not so long ago, when humankind
thought earth was the center of the entire universe. And a relatively simple universe it was. Earth was the only thing of its
kind—massive and multifaceted. The stars were nothing but
tiny points of light fixed in a great sphere wrapped around
Earth. The Sun and Moon were revolving light sources created
for Earth's service.

This is exactly as things appear to our vision. And when no
less a figure than Aristotle ratified it some four hundred years
B.C.E., it prevailed from ancient times until the seventeenth
century C.E., a span of two-thousand years.

The Scientific Revolution

Then Galileo, following Copernicus, said he had solid evidence the map was wrong. The Sun was really the center of the universe, it was bigger than Earth, and Earth was just one among a number of planets revolving around it. An uproar ensued. Galileo's portrait of things seemed an affront to humankind's dignity. And it bore no resemblance to the biblical account of creation. The Roman Catholic Church told Galileo he was plainly wrong and should speak no more. But the evidence was irrefutable, and it was only a matter of time before Galileo's view displaced its predecessor. Pope John Paul II recently apologized to Galileo for the church's mistaken condemnation, a mere four-hundred years after the fact.

At any rate, by the time Galileo, Copernicus, Francis Bacon, Huygens, Kepler, Pascal, Descartes, Boyle, and Newton had finished their work in the seventeenth century, we lived in quite a different universe. It was a great machine, consisting of bodies in motion, ranging in size from atoms to celestial giants, all moving according to fixed laws of nature. These laws had been uncovered and expressed in mathematical formulae during a century of remarkable scientific genius. God, the universe's Maker for those who still believed, stood outside it; it seemed to run quite well on its own. It was like a giant watch, God the brilliant and now largely idle Watchmaker.

Our Present Picture of the Universe

The picture has changed again.[1] The new conception takes nothing away from what these men said, but now knows that they were working on only the tiniest corner of what we now recognize the universe to be. The Sun, to which Earth compares in size as a marble to a beach ball, is just an average-sized star and is not the center of anything. It is one of between ten and one hundred billion stars in a galaxy called the Milky Way. There are billions of other galaxies as well, with like numbers of stars.

Billion is a word so commonly heard now, especially where federal expenditures are discussed, that it seems a thoroughly domesticated number. But it is no small quantity. If someone started a business in the year 1 C.E. with a capital of one billion dollars, and lost one thousand dollars a day, they would still be in business. In fact, they would have exhausted only two-thirds of their capital. Between ten and one hundred billion stars in the Milky Way....Billions of similar galaxies....What is Earth? One small planet revolving around one average-sized star in one of those billions of galaxies. Hmmm. If people were angry at Galileo for seeming to remove humanity from the throne, they should really be mad at those who pursued the investigation.

Yet even with that utterly staggering number of enormous bodies, space is nearly empty, so great are the distances between the stars. Our own Sun, much, much closer to us than any other star, is ninety-three million miles away. That is a fair bit of space. But the *next* nearest star is twenty-six million million miles away. To put it more scientifically, a light year is the distance light travels in a year, moving at a speed of 186,000 miles per second. The dimensions of the Milky Way are one hundred thousand light years by ten thousand. And that is just one galaxy. The universe is obviously impossible to portray. It is almost impossible to imagine.

Then there is the consideration of time. It was not until the beginning of the twentieth century that Darwin introduced us to the realization that the animals of Earth have evolved, from very simple organisms all the way to our very complex human selves. People resisted Darwin as vigorously as they had resisted Galileo. Now we know that Darwin was right, but that he too was working on just a tiny corner of reality. It is not just the animals, but the entire universe that has evolved. It has very gradually developed into what it is, and it continues to develop into we know not what.

Science has nearly reached consensus around what is called the Big Bang Theory of cosmic origins. The universe started from a tiny bit of matter/energy, about a millionth of a gram, incredibly dense and power packed. About fifteen billion years ago it exploded, like a balloon expanding outward, to form our present curved and still expanding galactic reality. Our Sun came to be about five billion years ago, Earth about four billion. To give us some sense of where humanity stands on that line of time, Carl Sagan once explained that if the universe's fifteen billion years were compressed into the span of a single calendar year, all recorded human history would be the last ten seconds of December 31, and the birth of Jesus would have occurred just two seconds before midnight. Human history sometimes seems long to us, especially when we go back to study ancient civilizations. But in the story of the universe, "ancient" human civilizations are fresh as a newborn babe.

So we are made of what the stars are made of, and from them we came. We have gotten a good deal more complicated in composition than the stars, but that has taken a very long time. And humankind is just one kind, helping to constitute a very complex and interdependent planetary reality. In a square foot of ordinary topsoil an inch deep, there lurk "an average of 1,356 living creatures...including 865 mites, 265 springtails, 22 millipedes, 19 adult beetles, and various numbers of 12 other forms..." (not to mention the microscopic population that would include up to two billion bacteria and millions of fungi, protozoa, and algae).[2]

It is all from the stars, mere hydrogen and helium though they be. In fact, it is all from that tiny speck of matter/energy that exploded outward fifteen billion years ago and is still expanding, the galaxies hurtling further apart from one another, and all of this matter/energy still organizing itself into more complex forms. Scientists now concede there is a very good chance of intelligent life on other planets in this vast cosmos. What kind of life? Who knows? Are there other universes as well? Perhaps. We do not know.

We have been speaking of the macrocosm. Let us descend to the microcosm, the atom, supposedly the ultimate building block of all that is, a unit of matter so tiny no microscope can see it. When I studied physics in college, the atom had been analyzed into three smaller components: protons and neutrons constituting a nucleus, and electrons revolving around that nucleus. Since then, several further types of minute particles have been found within the atom. The atom is now recognized to be a beehive of activity and energy, a cluster of vibrant relationships expressed in perpetual movement. In fact, the atom seems alive, a tiny organism. Atoms organize themselves into more complex organisms—into molecules, cells, plants, animals, humans. But even when they organize themselves into mere desks and chairs, if we could see what these inert, stolid objects really are, we would be contemplating a teeming mass of energized relationships in relentless action. Desk and chair are alive too, and dancing. So are the mountains.

Another discovery about the atom is that the classical division into matter (particles) and energy is not nearly as neat as it once seemed. Matter and energy convert back and forth inside the atom, the one into the other. The so-called particles of matter are really just tighter energy packets, the energy just matter more widely diffused. In fact, in science's present conception of reality, energy has replaced matter as the primary reality—no small revolution in conception. The world may look and feel like matter, but it is actually all energy. The great scientist Max Planck writes:

> As a man who has devoted his whole life to the most clear-headed science, to the study of matter, I can tell, as a result of my research about the atoms, this much: *there is no matter as such*. All matter originates and exists only by virtue of a force which brings the particles of an atom to vibration and holds the most minute solar system of the atom together.[3]

What emerges from all of this is a vision of reality as organism. From microscopic to macroscopic level, it is all alive, organisms within organisms within organisms. Even the totality, the vast universe, seems to be a single organism. In the words of philosopher/scientist Alfred North Whitehead,

> The field is now open for the introduction of some new doctrine of organism which may take the place of the materialism with which, since the seventeenth century, science has saddled philosophy.[4]

The universe, in other words, is not terribly different from our own body. Constituted of diverse members, yet all unity and interdependence, everything in either organism affects and is affected by everything else. On the human level, gangrene in a limb will soon kill the entire organism. Sexual arousal is genitally concentrated, but suffuses the entire body. Obesity will eventually ruin a part—knee, ankle, or heart. We now know planet Earth as a similar ecosystem. Eliminate one set of members, a species, for instance, and you destroy several others. Ruin the quality of air or water, and countless members of the total organism are destroyed. Decimate the forests, and watch the ensuing death of entire animal species, along with flood and thin air. Let the ozone layer be thinned or broken, and the entire body suffers sunburn. Writer David Toolan acquaints us with a dimension of human interdependence we seldom think of:

> Each time we breathe, we take in a quadrillion atoms breathed by the rest of humanity within the last two weeks and more than a million atoms breathed personally by each person on earth.[5]

And where the whole earth is concerned, we now recognize that humanity must honor its proper place in the entire system of things, or it will ruin both the delicate balance essential for the life of the planet, and itself in the process.

The cosmos itself is now likewise seen to be a single organism. It is harder at first to conceive of it as such because of the apparent lifelessness of its billions of burning hydrogen/helium masses, its many clumpish planets and meteors, and its vast empty spaces. How can this be a living thing? But an analogous "structure" runs the gamut from small to large. The atom itself is mostly empty space. Between its miniscule bits of "matter" lie immense distances, relatively speaking. And the human body, despite its solid appearance to our perception, is likewise mostly empty space, constituted entirely of these atom-universes of orbiting bitlets. The key to understanding nature at all levels is the discovery that from atomic to cosmic level, all these "empty spaces" are really energy fields teeming with activity, charged with the dynamic relationships and interplay between the more solid components. *All is live!*

It is clear that we have undergone another paradigm shift in the way we see the universe. Raised on the seventeenth century's view of a well-ordered machine consisting of material bodies in motion according to universal laws, we are being reborn now into a universe not only far vaster, but qualitatively different as well, a universe of organism in evolution. Where science used to find a book of laws, it now finds a story being told, an unfolding drama in which some restless primordial energy pushes things forward with remarkable creativity. There is spontaneity and unpredictability along with regularity, as in any human story. Nature exhibits an abundance of exceptions to what used to be thought of as binding laws. How the tale will end, nobody knows. In any case, the metaphor of a developing story has supplanted the older model of a mechanism governed by laws as the best description of what we now know the universe to be.

I have sketched this contemporary scientific picture of our universe because, as philosopher/scientist Alfred North Whitehead points out:

> The mentality of an epoch springs from the view of the world which is, in fact, dominant in the educated sections of the communities in question.[6]

While many people are not yet acquainted with this scientific picture, certainly not in its details, yet we catch its impact in many expressions drifting through our culture. And they will grow. Thus, what begins as esoteric and the property of a few gradually becomes commonplace, widely understood at least in outline and then taken for granted. A writer who answered my questionnaire describes his experience of God in today's universe:

I see a lot of effects of God's wisdom, astonishing harmony, breath-taking detail in human cell activity, the regularity of subatomic forces, the unspeakable breadth of the cosmos all hanging together: magnetism, chemistry, systems of life beginning and ending—all mixed with seemingly unanswerable questions and absurdities and apparently gratuitous cruelties: but after it all passes by, I choose (like Job) to submit, to surrender. I cover my mouth.

Since our feel for the universe strongly affects our religious conceptions, we are religiously in transition too. In fact, we are undergoing a *major* shift in our thinking about what lies at the base of reality, what we usually call "God." How do those most expert in the matter, theologians, think about God today? This brings us to the next chapter.

Questions and Exercises

1. As you have become gradually educated since you were a child about the universe you live in, what, if anything, has happened to your image of yourself and your place in the total scheme of things? What has happened to your image of God?

2. Try the idea of organism on some smaller-scale realities: a garden, a forest, a family, an athletic team. Does it fit? Does the conception of the universe as a huge single organism make sense to you? How can there be organism (unity, inter-dependence, vitality) where there are such vast distances and such a variety of supposed constituents?

Chapter Two

God Needs a New Description, a New Location, and a New Name

> What is the right way to speak about God? This is a question of unsurpassed importance, for speech to and about the mystery that surrounds human lives and the universe itself is a key activity of a community of faith.
>
> —*Elizabeth Johnson*

The word *God* is a fascinating one. Even people within the same religious tradition mean very different things by it. Today, many intelligent people hesitate to speak of God at all, because they can no longer believe in God—the God, that is, that they were raised with. They would not call themselves atheists, and are often quite interested in spirituality, but the God of their childhood has faded from view entirely and nothing more adequate has come to replace "Him." When they think about it, they wonder if they believe at all.

A great deal of the difficulty, I submit, lies in the way God is understood, imaged, and located. These are typically so at variance with our lived experience that "He" is incredible, irrelevant, or both.

The God of our Christian childhood is a Father Figure in the skies. This image may be useful in giving children some initial sense of what we mean by God. But as we mature, and our experience and knowledge expand, it becomes increasingly problematic. Yet it is kept very much alive in our adult churches—in the language of the readings, the prayers, and the preaching—so much so that some refer to God in casual conversation as "the man upstairs." Such imagery may once have fit humankind's map of the universe. Today, it is for large numbers of people simply an unnecessary stumbling block to faith.

Part of the anachronistic imagery depicts what this Father in the sky is doing. Not very much. Mostly sitting there, blissful in Trinitarian life, surrounded by angels and saints, benignly overseeing things on earth. And he might as well, for his created world runs quite well on its own. He has only to maintain it, observe human beings' behavior for future reward and punishment, and make small interventions in human affairs either in answer to prayers or in immediate punishment of wicked deeds.

It is hard to stay interested in this God, people are finding today. It is also difficult to establish any real connection. We sometimes go to church to renew contact, read scriptural accounts of God's deeds past, perform the familiar ritual again in quest of some sort of communion. But daily demands soon draw our attention to matters more pressing, the arduous business of survival in the world. And if amid our toil we observe human affairs closely, we run up against considerable difficulty with the doctrine that this God above answers prayers and punishes the wicked. The wicked seem to be doing fine, and a great many prayers get no apparent answer.

A New Location

First, we are looking in the wrong place. God is not up there. There is no *up* anymore; there is only *out*. But God is not out there either—except insofar as God pervades the whole universe. What pertains to us more closely and must touch us more compellingly is that God is *here*, animating our environment. God is *within*, within all things. The place to look is not up but *down*, deep down. When we touch the depths, we touch God. I mean both the depth of all that is around us and the depth of our own self. I also mean the depth of our relationships.

Contemporary Protestant theologian Paul Tillich put it this way:

> The name of this infinite and inexhaustible depth and ground of all being is *God*. That depth is what the word *God* means. And if that word has not much meaning for you, translate it, and speak of the depths of your life, of the source of your being, of your ultimate concern, of what you take seriously without any reservation. Perhaps, in order to do so, you must forget everything traditional that you have learned about God, perhaps even that word itself. For if you know that God means depth, you know much about Him [*sic*]. You cannot then call yourself an atheist or unbeliever. For you cannot think or say: Life has no depth! Life itself is shallow. Being itself is surface only. If you could say this in complete seriousness, you would be an atheist; but otherwise you are not.[1]

Suppose we express Tillich's wonderful insight in the language of the contemporary scientific picture. If the universe is an organism, God is its soul. God dwells within the world, animating it.

I speak analogously here, metaphorically rather than literally. Christian theology has always spoken of God's *transcendence* and *immanence*, and still does. The immanence part means that God is deep within all things. The transcendence part means that God is at the same time beyond it all, not to be identified with it. You can analyze nature down to its finest components, and you will never find God. Unfortunately, the notion of transcendence has often led to people locating God outside the system, above it. What it really means is simply that God is not a part of the system of things, but the mystery at its source. That is where the metaphor of the soul in the body comes in. Imagine an invisible center of energy, vitality, creativity, and love at the core of everything, and you have a good sense of what we mean by God.

While there is nothing wrong with saying that God is a *person*, I find it more helpful to say that God is *personal*. As soon as we say a *person*, we imagine a body, even if it be a spiritual body. And then we have to find a place for it. That is how God gets "up there," or "out there," alongside the world rather than inside it. And that is the mistake. If we just say that God is *personal*, that is, that the Source of all reality knows and relates so that we can have an I-Thou relationship with It, we have expressed the essential truth without causing ourselves problems.

In contemporary theology, God did not simply create the world. The world is a process, and God is always both creating and animating it. Though it be several billion years old, the cosmos is quite possibly still in its merest youth, with most of its life stretching before it. Who knows the full story God is slowly writing, what the ultimate realization of the divine vision might be? At any rate, on this reading God is still fully engaged with the cosmos, not occasionally intervening in it, but rather indwelling it as its soul, expressing the divine self in the universe's life and its upward movement toward full realization.

Reflecting on the new science's implications for theology, Jesuit Father David Toolan remarks:

> Moreover, as Northrop Frye once observed, to begin to think of God in the way scientists now do of atoms and electrons—as forces, fields, and energies rather than "things,"—may prove a way of recovering our biblical ancestors' sense that God is linguistically a "word of power," not a noun but essentially verb.[2]

What applies to the whole applies also to the part, and so to me, blip on the screen though I be. God dwells in me as well. God animates me. God is still creating me too, both from within and from without. When I go deep inside, there I find the Quiet Presence. The more I am in touch with my personal center, the more I am in touch with God.

This view of God as soul of the world has important ramifications for ecology, our sense of self, contemplation, and public prayer.

1. If the world is the body of God, it is all sacred space. We stand on holy ground, and, like Moses, might well take off our shoes. All things, living and nonliving, deserve our deepest reverence and respect. This is exactly the sense Native American spirituality has always had. Once we catch the vision, there can be no more rape of the earth. A story from the ancient wisdom tradition comes to mind.[3]

> Once upon a time there was a forest where the birds sang by day and the crickets by night. Trees flourished, flowers bloomed, and all manner of creatures roamed in freedom. And all who entered there were led to wonder and worship, for they felt the presence of God.

21

Then the Age of Unconsciousness dawned, when it became possible for people to construct buildings a thousand feet high, and to destroy rivers and forests and mountains. And houses of worship were built from the wood of the forest and the rock of the mountain. Flowers were brought inside, water was placed in fonts, and bells replaced the sounds of Nature. And God suddenly had a much smaller home.

2. We too are holy somehow, in spite of ourselves, for God dwells in us. If one of the effects of our new awareness of the vastness of the universe is to expand our sense of God's immensity, another is to deepen our amazement that each of us can still have a personal relationship with this God. It is not only possible, it is our deepest destiny, the very thing we were made for. And the One we seek lives not at a distance, but already inside us. In St. Paul's expression, we are temples of the Spirit (1 Cor 6:19).

3. These two points lay the basis for the practice of contemplation. Contemplation is first a deeper seeing, and then a reverent response naturally stirred by what one sees. God is the soul of the world, showing and giving self in all that is. God is in the tree I see, giving it life, growth, and grace; in the bowl of soup I eat, giving it flavor and nutrition; in the face of the person I love, source of his or her beauty and goodness. Contemplation is this deeper vision into things, and the resultant reverence. It is a form of prayer available all day long, right in the midst of the hurly burly. But God is inside me as well, source of my life, creativity, and love. So I can close my eyes, shut out the world, and commune with God at the center of my being. Eastern contemplation has tended by and large to go inward, Western outward. Both approaches

are valid. A surgeon who answered my questionnaire recounts a meeting with the Holy in medical school:

> We did an embryology experiment, the gestation of a chicken in 21 days. We had 21 chicken eggs which had been fertilized on the same day. One egg was carefully opened each day for the following 21 days. It was a most dramatic experience, to view the formation of the chicken starting from amorphous egg yolk to new life of enormous complexity. The process was orderly and segmented, as dividing and differentiating cells formed the various organ systems—heart, lungs, skeleton, GI tract, etc. It was awesome.

A therapist describes the other form of contemplation, going within:

> I meditate every morning—deep breathing exercises—contact with my body, my sensations, my feelings—that brings me to my deeper self, the void, where God is. Also, I have a few good friends with whom I can discuss my real inner experience. Our sharing is community. And in that community is God.

4. Public prayer should direct us to where God really is, not up but down deep. Then we could inhabit the world more perceptively. "We walk through mysteries, as a child scuffles through daisies," the saying goes. So not just two sacraments, nor even seven, but an unlimited number, because *all* things are charged with the grandeur of God. Not just one book of sacred stories, but as many sacred stories as there are human stories. Not just the church space, its symbols and rites, and its ordained presider as holy, but the entire motley assembly,

filled with the presence and activity of God and equally worthy of reverence. Either our religious assemblies insistently remind us of what is far greater than ourselves and always present and active in the whole world, or they do us the disservice of shrinking our vision and confining our souls in a cramped space.[4]

Yes, God needs a new location. Our scientific vision of the universe, and even our daily experience, compel us to move God from the skies above and from the church on the corner to the heart and center of all reality.

A New Description

I believe in God. But what do I mean by that word *God*? I no longer believe in the Father in the skies, the God I was raised with. Years ago I began feeling the need for a new description, one better corresponding to my actual experience of God. Of course this experience is not unique to me. Many other people also have it, and so in what follows I use "we" language. What I want to do is try to put the ordinary, daily experience of God into words. Here are eight ways to give meaning to the word *God*, based on experiences available to us all.

1. *God is the Source of reality*. Every morning we wake up again to the mystery of the world. Why is there something rather than nothing? And look at all there is. By the word *God* we mean whatever animates, empowers, nourishes, renews reality. The question about God is the question about whether the world we know just is, without cause or explanation, or is grounded in a source that might explain it. Believing in God means believing there is something more than meets the eye, something behind or within what we immediately encounter.

24

2. God is the Object of our deepest longing. It is hard to conceptualize or even imagine this object of our longing, but we know the longing well. And we know that nothing we have been able to find satisfies our restless discontent. It is there even in the best of times. And in times less good, Hamlet's words find a deep resonance in us:

> O, that this too too solid flesh would melt,
> thaw, and resolve itself into a dew!
> Or that the Everlasting had not fixed
> His canon 'gainst self-slaughter. O God! O God!
> How weary, stale, flat, and unprofitable
> Seem to me all the uses of this world!
> Fie on 't! O fie! 'Tis an unweeded garden
> That grows to seed; things rank and gross in nature
> Possess it merely. (Hamlet I, 2)

This feeling of being unhappy in the world, of being at some level always dissatisfied with everything, this constant "transcendence of the human spirit," as Karl Rahner calls it, such that we are at the party and not at the party at the same time, points toward the true object of our longing—something obviously beyond all that is immediately given. That Object, featureless though it be in our awareness, is another description of what we mean by the word *God*. Its relevance is obvious from the ache of our emptiness.

3. God is the Assurance of meaning, value, purpose. Without God, we are by no means sure of these things, crucial though they be. Life puzzles us profoundly. At times it seems altogether meaningless. A woman, fifty-two, puts it this way:

> Personally, what I am seeking is answers to all life's major
> questions: How can we find the strength to continue to

struggle against the sometimes evil and more often pervasive indifference of most human beings to the sufferings
of others outside their immediate circle? What can be
done with the rage generated by the feelings of frustration
at the fundamental injustices in the human condition? On
a micro-level, I long for something that will help me cope
with the inevitable losses that accompany aging....I have
no vision of what spirituality could mean for me. I only
know that the resources upon which I have relied to cope
with life's travails to this point will not work when con-
fronted with the ultimate realities....

God is the Guarantor of meaning and value. This does not
mean that if we believe, we will know and understand the
meaning and value. But one of the crucial differences belief in
God makes is that even when we cannot see the meaning or
value of our lives (or of someone else's, or of the world's), we
remain convinced of it in faith. We believe that God is good, has
a plan, and is dedicated to realizing that plan. As the popular
hymn puts it, "He's got the whole world in his hands."

Faith knows that God's thoughts are beyond our thoughts,
God's ways beyond our ways (Is 55:8). Job, to take a famous
biblical case, doesn't understand God at all. Convinced that he
has always lived a good life, he cannot fathom why his fortunes
have gone so sour. He rails at God, demands a meeting. When
God finally "speaks to" Job, God does not explain anything to
him. God merely points to the wonders of creation, phenomena
beyond Job's compass, in this way hinting how far beyond Job's
understanding are God's thoughts and ways (Jb 38). Though
Job grasps not a whit more of what he demanded to know, he
comes away from the encounter strangely comforted. There is
obviously much more to the mystery of it all than his little mind
can grasp.

4. *God is the Depth in things, the Mystery in the background.* Where is God in our day-to-day experience? Always at the edges of our awareness. God is the Horizon of all our experience, the Mystery in the background, Karl Rahner tells us. Very rarely do we focus on the horizon, but always we are viewing objects against its backdrop, so always it is at the edges of awareness. God is like that. It is against the background of God that we apprehend the particularity and inadequacy of everything we encounter in this world. Paul Tillich, as we have seen, offers a slightly different metaphor, but it too points to the constant though unobtrusive presence of God to us. God is the Depth in things, Tillich says. We can skim the surfaces of life, and often do, especially when we are running to get things done, running away from ourselves, running with the throng. Then we have little sense of God—yet even then, God is dimly in awareness because God is in the depths. When we slow down and are more attuned to the depths, we are more God-aware.

5. *God is the Power on which we rely.* In desperate situations, we call on that power instinctively, even those of us who rarely advert to God. We call out to whatever can save us or help us when we feel our smallness and weakness. A couple getting married want a blessing, because they know marriage is a daunting venture and they are afraid. If they do not think in terms of a blessing, they are careful to date their wedding under a propitious constellation of planets and stars, simply another way of expressing their felt need for the assistance of greater powers. Before a job interview, a public performance, a birth, we can hardly resist calling on *Something* for help. Anyone who joins AA or one of its spin-off groups to overcome an addiction, begins by admitting that he or she has become powerless in the face of the addiction, and needs the help of a "Higher Power" to accomplish what seems impossible. This is another of the

regular indications of what "God" is to us: that Power on which we instinctively call when we feel our limitations. When you ask people to tell of their religious experiences, many will tell you of God's majesty in the mountain, the sunset, the ocean. We somehow forget how often we have encountered God when we were desperate, out of options, at the bottom of the pit.

6. *God is the Font of beauty, goodness, truth, love.* God is, of course, the source of everything. But by widely flung testimony, in beauty, goodness, truth, and love, God's presence is especially evident. Instinctively we regard these things with respect and admiration. With special eloquence they proclaim something behind or within them. The depths open up. We pause. We are in the presence of the Holy. Take love, for example. A husband and father writes:

> I experience God in the daily, mundane involvement with my kids. The fun they have, the strange things they say take me out of myself and into an experience of joy that is uncreated and unimagined. I experience God in loving and being loved by my wife. There is something in this committed way of living that connects with a God who is faithful.

7. *God is the Silent Presence deep within us.* Deep inside us, well below the surface of our ordinary consciousness and usual mental activity is a place incredibly still, like a small chapel. Here is another locus of the encounter, at the core of our being. We do not often visit this place, though it is really a delightful one to spend time in. There lives a Quiet Presence there, very refreshing to be with.

But can we stand just being, and just being with, conditioned as we are to perpetual activity? Will we quickly leave because God is not saying anything to us? Will we give up because our mind, which has a life of its own and never stops churning, pulls us quickly out of this sanctuary to more mundane concerns? If we can be patient, and keep gently returning to this sanctuary every time our thoughts fly away, and if we can let God be God and not push for anything, there is no place quite so pleasant to be, no Presence quite so wonderful to sit with. A woman writes:

> One of the greatest religious experiences that I've had is experiencing the light of my inner self—"the kingdom of God is within"—especially in the presence of a great teacher, such as Gurumaji Childvilasananda.

8. *God is the Call to do the good, to be responsible*. Something inside us keeps prompting us to do the good. We have a strong sense that we must do certain things and must not do certain others. It feels like a nudge, a push, sometimes a pull. It is an inner movement, a felt sense. We can go against it and sometimes do, but when we do we feel bad, as if we have failed in something important. Cardinal John Henry Newman called this inner urge conscience, and it was for him one of the strongest indications of God's presence within us.

Here we have a way in which God works with us constantly. And there seems to be no interaction of greater significance, because our responses here determine what kind of person we are making of ourselves. Even at those times of our lives when God seems distant or absent, when beauty and goodness touch us not, when life seems meaningless and our inner sanctuary empty, there remain the good we must do and the evil we must avoid. It is spiritual bedrock. An older woman's testimony bears this out:

I pray he is there, but I don't "feel" him being there. Sometimes I'm even afraid we've made him up. I don't know. Sometimes I want to quit, but there is no other way. There's nothing else to do. I try to grow spiritually because I have to, God or no God. There is nothing else. Mindfulness. Being the best I can be.

If you look back over all these descriptions of what we mean by God, you can see that they are all somewhat vague, vague not in the sense that the experience or the idea lack substance, but in the sense that no clear image of God emerges. There is no body, nor even a face. There is a definite activity toward us, an influence upon us; but the source of them remains hidden. We respond without knowing what we are responding to. God is invisible. God is mystery. So in speaking thus indeterminately of God, we are just being true to our experience, respectful of it. And that is the hallmark of all these descriptions of the Sacred: they are rooted in our ordinary, everyday experience of life in the world.

The Judaeo-Christian tradition confirms us. It has always held that God is Spirit. The Hindu, Muslim, and Native American traditions are in complete agreement. Native Americans have always simply and aptly called God "The Great Spirit." Spirit cannot be drawn. It is difficult even to describe. We know it only from its influence and effect.

But this raises a crucial question. What is the relationship between these nebulous descriptions of God stemming from experience, and Yahweh of the Jewish tradition, or the Father of the Christian tradition? As soon as we introduce those names, we can feel the difference. We have just moved from the vague to the clearly delineated. It is almost as if we have moved from the invisible to the visible. For we have seen *pictures* of Yahweh, pictures of Jesus' Father. They have definite features, and strong personality traits. In fact, they look like *us*, only, of course, bigger, stronger, smarter.

Yahweh and the Father of Jesus are *images* of God. They are, in fact, the operative images of God for vast numbers of people. The great advantage they have over the vaguer descriptions above is that, precisely by giving the Mystery features, they make it in some ways more real and easier to relate to. Shakespeare describes it this way:

> The poet's eye, in a fine frenzy rolling,
> Doth glance from heaven to earth, from earth to heaven,
> And, as imagination bodies forth
> The forms of things unknown, the poet's pen
> Turns them to shapes, and gives to airy nothing
> A local habitation and a name.
>
> *(A Midsummer Night's Dream, V, 1)*

The Bible is the work of religious poets, who give the Spirit of human religious experience a local habitation and a name. While we are indebted to them for this heightened feature, there are drawbacks too. Such images diminish the Mystery, sometimes almost domesticate it, stress some of its aspects much more than others, and run the risk, especially with the stories that cluster around them, of being childish, foreign to evolving experience, and hence incredible. Today's "loss of faith" has much more to do with these images of God than it does with the reality of the Mystery and people's experience of it.

Thinking of God as Spirit has as much biblical warrant as thinking of God as King or Father, though these latter images have become much more dominant in Christian thinking. But before the Christian doctrine of Trinity was elaborated in the fourth and fifth centuries and Spirit became just an aspect of God, Spirit *was* God and God was Spirit. The Spirit that brooded over the waters at creation, the Spirit which descended on the king and spoke through the prophets, the Spirit which filled Jesus at his baptism, the Spirit which empowered the first Christians was simply God. In this Spirit-model God is imaged as a nonmaterial reality pervading the universe. And the etymology of the Hebrew word for Spirit, *ruach*, is richly descriptive of God, for it means both wind and breath. Wind and breath are both invisible, yet potent. The one completely surrounds us, the other goes in and out of us. What wonderful images for God. In many ways it is unfortunate that this Spirit-model for God has been so eclipsed by the Monarchical-model in religious discourse.[5]

A New Name

The word *God* has come to mean so many different things, it sometimes seems we should scrap it altogether and start over. The point is illustrated in a dialogue I had with a man who was raised Christian, threw it all over as he entered adulthood, then later joined AA when he had fallen victim to alcohol and drugs.

> "It's really obvious, as you talk, how much God has come to mean to you."

> "I'm sorry, but I don't believe in God. I've put my whole life now in the hands of my Higher Power."

> "I see. OK, can I just ask though, when you say you don't believe in God, what is it that you don't believe in?"

> "The Christian God. A God who puts out all kinds of rules, and judges and punishes, and only accepts people who meet certain religious requirements."

> "Well, I don't believe in that kind of God either. When I use the word *God*, I mean what you seem to mean when you say 'HP': I mean Someone who is all for you no matter who you are, who accompanies you and empowers you, who sticks with you even when you fail, like a good friend."

> "Oh. I can relate to that. But that is not at all the God I was taught."

This man does not believe in "God," yet his relationship with God is obviously the most important thing in his life. Should we just give the Mystery a new name, and start over? The proposal has been made more than once, but has somehow never carried. Who would know what the strange new term referred to? If we could get that cleared up, would everybody accept the new name? What would we do with all the sacred texts, songs, derivative writings, and other elements of the tradition based on the old name? And how would we prevent the new name from eventually suffering the same fate as the old?

Perhaps it is best to stick with the traditional name, and to work instead on refurbishing the *images* and *concepts* with which it is linked, making it clear in our conversation what we do and do not mean. In the section above where I attempted to describe how God impinges on our experience, I already used several names not too commonly employed: *Source, Assurance, Depth, Silence, Power, Horizon, Presence, Mystery.* There are other names of a similar sort: *Higher Power, the Sacred, the Holy, the Transcendent, Spirit.* Wouldn't it be refreshing to hear words like these sprinkled throughout the preaching, songs, and prayers of our religious gatherings instead of always "Father," "His," and "Him"? These one-word descriptive terms lie somewhere between images and concepts, not quite as concrete as images, not quite as abstract as concepts. They respect the transcendence of the Mystery, yet are closely tied to our experience.

If we want to image God more concretely, feminist theology is a fertile source.[6] It begins by pointing out the danger of idolatry in the way we have canonized the Father image. When just a single image is used in this way, we soon forget that it is just an image. We think God really is a male person. Not only does this diminish the richness of the Holy, it has harmful consequences as well. The Father God presents difficulties for those who have not had a good experience of their earthly fathers. The Male God easily becomes the ultimate sanction for patriarchy in church and society. And the Male God has often been the Warrior God, champion of his own people in Holy War.

Why not use equally legitimate metaphors for the God of our tradition, but ones that change our feel not only for God, but for one another and the earth? Theologian Sally McFague proposes three such images: *God the Mother, God the Lover, and God the Friend*. Each has biblical warrant. And each has a very different feel than *God the Father* has. A woman twenty-one, a student, writes of this different feel in recounting an experience she had of God as Friend:

> I was in a small chapel on one of the retreats sponsored by Campus Ministry, praying in front of the Blessed Sacrament. It was late at night and I was alone, just speaking out loud as if I was having a chat with an old friend. I was struck by a very peaceful, warm, and loving presence around me, and even after I was done "praying," I had great difficulty leaving that chapel.

McFague is also concerned about fostering a sense of the sacredness of earth and cosmos, and so she proposes speaking of them as the Body of God.[7] As we saw earlier, this imagery closes the gap between the Creator out in space and the planet on which we live. Immediately we have both a more sacred planet and a more involved God.

Rosemary Radford Ruether, seeing how God the Father is usually internalized as Paternal Superego, again changes the metaphor. Seeing and feeling the world as a woman does, Ruether says she instinctively thinks of God as the Empowering Matrix.[8] A *matrix* is that in which things are embedded and is a feminine noun in Latin. The matrix Ruether has in mind is filled with life and power, as if to say God is the fertile soil in which all things are rooted.

Feminist theologians stress the need for multiple images of God, reminding us that the Bible itself uses a multiplicity of images, some masculine, but some feminine, and some impersonal. Both the biblical writers and today's theologians are agreed on this: that for so rich a mystery as lies behind this universe, we need many images, not just one. There are so many facets of it to express.

God needs a new definition, a new location, and a new name. When the necessary alterations are made, there are not nearly as many "atheists." For God has become something both discoverable in experience and relevant to life.

Questions and Exercises

1. Has this chapter changed the way you think about God? If so, how?

2. The chapter named eight ways to give meaning to the word *God* based on experiences available to us all: Source of reality, Object of longing, Assurance of meaning, Depth in things or Horizon, Power on which we rely, Font of goodness, Silent Presence within, Call to do the good? Which of these experiences of God do you most relate to? Would you add others?

3. As between the monarchical model for God and the spirit model, which do you feel more drawn to and why?

4. Try praying for a week with an image of God as Mother, or as Lover, or as Friend. Journal about the difference it makes in the way you feel toward God, yourself, and the spiritual life.

5. Try praying for a week with an image of God as wind and breath. Journal about this experience.

6. Ask a couple of your friends what their prevalent image of God is. Then check to see if they view it as just an image, or if they think God really is so.

Chapter Three
What Is "Spirituality"?

Spirituality is broader than a theology or set of
values precisely because it is so all-encompassing
and pervasive.

—*Anne Carr*

Paradoxically, the secular culture in which we live has suddenly become very interested in spirituality. Books on the topic are selling very well. Public radio and TV talk shows interview a new crop of spiritual authorities. Shops appear selling incense, crystals, and other paraphernalia of innovative spiritual practice. Workshops teaching methods of meditation, the enneagram, the chakras, and journaling draw large numbers of people. Continuing education events for physical and mental health professionals offer short courses on the use of hypnosis, guided visualization, and other ways of accessing inner powers for healing and wholeness. All of these diverse elements are gathered under a very broad umbrella called spirituality.

At the very least, the breadth and energy of the movement indicate a deep hunger in people for something more—something more than everything already being offered in a very prosperous culture.

For those of us formed in the religious tradition of Christianity there is a puzzlement here and a feeling of being slightly overwhelmed. In this chapter, let us see first if we can get a clearer grasp of what spirituality is. Then let us examine its relationship to religion. Finally, let us try to develop some perspectives that will help us contextualize today's spiritual offerings.

Can Spirituality Be Defined?

The heightened interest in spirituality has brought forward a host of definitions of the term. Not too long ago, a popular magazine put out a special inspirational issue, among other things, reporting back on some 2100 responses it had received to its spirituality questionnaire. It is remarkable that a popular magazine would treat spirituality at all, and that such a large number of readers would respond to its questionnaire on the topic, but such are the signs of the times. Respondents defined spirituality as follows:

> "Connection to a reality that is more than self and comforts and guides us"

> "Magical, innocent, like a child viewing things for the first time"

> "Belief in a higher power"

> "A connection to all living things and to the earth and universe"

> "The essence of a person's character without any material trapping"

Each of these responses offers some insight into the topic.

What Is "Spirituality"?

Persons who have made longer, more serious study of the matter offer these descriptions:[2]

> Psychiatrist Gerald May: "Spirituality refers to our deepest values and desires, the very core of our being."

> Psychologist Molly Brown: "When we expand our awareness, strengthen our center, clarify our purpose, transform our inner demons, develop our will and make conscious choices, we are moving toward deeper connection with our spiritual self."

> Spiritual writer John Shea: "The spiritual life is, at root, a matter of seeing...."

> Jungian therapist Jeremiah Abrams: "Spirituality is a holy longing, a yearning to know the meaning of our lives, to have a connection with the transpersonal."

> Theologian Kathleen Fischer: "Spirituality is how we express ourselves in relation to that which we designate as the source of ultimate power and meaning in life and how we live out this relationship. It may be a personal system or organized and institutionalized."

> Theologian Sandra Schneiders: "...the interest in spirituality...represents...a profound and authentic desire of twentieth-century humanity for wholeness in the midst of fragmentation, for community in the face of isolation and loneliness, for liberating transcendence, for meaning in life, for values that endure. Human beings are spirit in the world, and spirituality is the effort to understand and realize the potential of that extraordinary and paradoxical condition."

Here we have an even richer cluster of insights.

Is it not curious that so many differing descriptions of the same basic phenomenon are given? What does this mean? At the very least, it seems evident that spirituality is a deep, complex, many-sided reality not easily pulled into a simple, unified description. And perhaps, on reflection, that is little wonder. Look at what a multifaceted reality the human spirit, soul, or self is—how many capacities it has, and how many needs and wants. It can and does branch out in many different directions as it expresses itself and seeks what it desires.

Is there any way we can assemble all these descriptions into some sort of total vision? First, it is striking that spirituality has to do with the soul or core of the self, and that what is envisioned is some cultivation and enrichment of one's inner life. The interest in spirituality seems to originate in a felt need at the core of the self, and this is for several a good place to start the description. Second, many of the statements speak of another referent with which the soul seeks to enjoy a stronger relationship. It is variously named here—the transpersonal, Spirit, higher power, source of ultimate power and meaning. What is hinted at is somewhat vague, yet perceived as real and deemed important. Third, there is clear reference to quality of life as an expression of spirituality—meaning, direction, values, connection to all things. These three elements, common to most of the descriptions offered above, lead me to embrace yet another definition, one which was offered by Jesuit priest Steven Sundborg at an evening of renewal:

"Spirituality is our lived relationship with Mystery."

I like it for several reasons. It is very economical, easy to remember. Yet in its brief compass it seems to include all the vital elements. Its main focus is on life as lived, the chief expression of a person's spirituality. It clearly names Mystery (another name for God) as vital referent, source of the life lived out. And it at least alludes to the spiritual core of the person, the center, which is in relationship with God and directing the life that is lived. As we will see, at least in Christian spirituality, the one with which we are most familiar, from that I-Thou relationship at the core of one's existence there flow all the other elements of a total spirituality.

What are the elements of a total spirituality? In their book, *Spiritual Literacy: Reading the Sacred in Everyday Life*, Frederic and Mary Ann Brussat offer us a very eligible list. It is an alphabet of items to be attended to if you want to develop a spiritual life.[3]

A	Attention
B	Beauty/Being Present
C	Compassion/Connections
D	Devotion
E	Enthusiasm
F	Faith/Forgiveness
G	Grace/Gratitude
H	Hope/Hospitality
I	Imagination
J	Joy/Justice
K	Kindness
L	Listening/Love
M	Meaning
N	Nurturing
O	Openness
P	Peace/Play
Q	Questing
R	Reverence
S	Shadow/Silence

T	Teachers/Transformation
U	Unity
V	Vision
W	Wonder
X	The Mystery
Y	Yearning/You
Z	Zeal

Though it is not a definition, this list abundantly conveys what spirituality is. It catalogues the immense possibilities of the human spirit. Item for item, it is an inventory worth attending to, whatever one's spiritual persuasion. Each entry arrests attention. How, I wonder, am I doing at that? How might my life change if I made a serious practice of this? The register is remarkably comprehensive, almost worth memorizing. I can think of a few items I might add: ritual, meditation, beliefs, discernment, perhaps. But I like the entries already at those letters. Then I notice that the authors themselves have double entries at several letters, so they could probably handle additions. At any rate, the list manages, under the strictures of an alphabetical grid, to lay out most if not all the essential ingredients of a genuine spirituality. It is evident that spirituality is a whole way of life, a vital factor operative all day every day. To catch the impact of this alphabet is to realize what a profound challenge real spiritual living is. Yet it all sounds very attractive too, which points up another truth: at a deep level we want to be spiritual. There is something about a lived relationship with Mystery that grabs us.

Spirituality and Religion

What is the relationship between spirituality and religion? When Benedictine Father Bede Griffiths, who spent most of his life in India and was revered there as a guru, was asked this question in an interview in 1993, he held up his hand to the audience:

> The fingers are the religions, but they all come together in the palm, their source. This is the distinction between religion and spirituality.

Spirituality is prior to religion. It is religion's root. Our relationship with Mystery, as we saw in the last chapter, is a given in life, or at least it is a constant offer. Spirit is the Wind all around us, the Breath we breathe in and out. Since the Mystery is present to us always, we need not go to church to find It or even to cultivate our relationship with It.

Yet the spiritual person might well embrace a religion, because religion supports and nourishes spirituality. It institutionalizes it. Churches, mosques, temples, and synagogues are *spirituality centers.* They exist precisely to cultivate spiritual living. They are certainly not without their faults, but they possess copious resources for nurturing the spiritual life. The key to understanding the mysterious mix of helpful and unhelpful elements in organized religion is to recognize how institutionalization works.

We institutionalize whatever is valuable enough to us that we want to preserve it. The process is gradual; at first we do not even realize we are doing it. Suppose a group of people enjoys getting together to play bridge. The first time or two it happens, it just happens. But if they really enjoy it, they will take steps to ensure it keeps going by making some agreements. They will decide how often they will meet and where. They might arrange to rotate play among their homes. As they play on, they will start making rules in answer to questions that arise. They will probably start keeping records. Customs will develop, like serving food and drink. These too become "rules," so that if the host failed to serve according to custom, everyone would remark on the way home, "Isn't it strange that they didn't serve anything but…?" Soon the question of admitting new members will probably arise and be decided one way or another. Certain tasks will gradually be defined and assigned to certain people, who now have established roles to play. After the group has met several times, they will have developed a modest tradition. And so on. You can observe the same thing among people who gather to clean up litter, to read and discuss books, to start a small business. In fact, you can see it in your own family, because every family is an institution too, with its roles, rules, and traditions. It could even write a mission statement, though, thankfully, most do not.

Institutionalization is a mixed bag. You can see the mix more easily in a religion than in a family. The original inspiration, which so enlivened the first members of a religion, can wane with time, and the group carries on more by the letter than by the spirit. Roles and rules become rigid, poorly serving changing needs. Leadership can become corrupt, more bent now on enjoying the personal advantages of power than on serving the common good. Traditions easily ossify, and the community keeps doing things simply because "this is the way we have always done it." There is a wonderful little story on this item from the wisdom tradition:

> When the guru sat down to worship each evening, the ashram cat would get in the way and distract the worshipers. So he ordered that the cat be tied during evening worship.

Long after the guru died, the cat continued to be tied during evening worship. And when the cat eventually died, another cat was brought to the ashram so that it could be duly tied during evening worship.

Centuries later learned treatises were written by the guru's disciples on the essential role of a cat in all properly conducted worship.

Now let us reflect for a moment on how a whole religion begins. Rosemary Radford Ruether charts it this way, citing Walter Otto: "First the god, then the dance, and finally the story."[5] That is how she sets forth religion's foundational elements. First comes someone's theophany or religious experience. Then come dance and drama, a ritual for making the god present again and reenacting the experience for the community. Then comes the story, the telling of the original experience, which is often incorporated into the ritual or liturgy. Finally comes theology, which is reflection on the whole and its organized formulation into teachings or doctrines. Theology is obviously at some distance from the spiritual experience that gave rise to the entire process, which is just to say again that spirituality precedes religion and is its vital root. A religion begins from the religious experience of a great seer, who has some profound sort of vision.[6] This seer, a spiritual giant, relatively, enjoying a much more lively relationship with the Mystery than most of us do, naturally attracts disciples (literally, "learners") who want more of what he or she has. Now you have a small community and, inevitably, institutionalization begins. Eventually the original seer dies, but the religion lives on. The wisdom tradition offers another timely story, pointing up a danger at this juncture in the process of transmission.

The mystic was back from the desert. "Tell us," they avidly said. "What is God like?"

But how could she ever put into words what she had experienced? Is it possible to put Truth into words?

She finally gave them a formula—so inaccurate, so inadequate—in the hope that some of them might be tempted, through it, to experience for themselves what she had experienced.

They seized upon the formula. They made a sacred text out of it. They imposed it upon everyone as a holy belief. They went to great pains to spread it in foreign lands. Some even gave their lives for it.

The mystic was sad. "It might have been better if I had never spoken," she mused.

Before leaving this section on spirituality, we might just remark that until recently, Christians did not use the term *spirituality* very much. Take Roman Catholics, for instance. What did we used to call what we now call spirituality? We called it our religion, our faith life, the following of Christ, the imitation of Christ, discipleship, or simply the Christian life. When we used the term *spirituality*, we had something more specific in mind. We spoke of Franciscan spirituality, or Jesuit spirituality, by which we meant the particular emphases St. Francis, St. Ignatius, or other Christian exemplars put on the various components of the Christian life. The Christian life had long been earnestly lived in consecrated communities of religious women and men, and that is where most of the spiritual practice was developed on which the whole church drew, various approaches to the Christian life that were called spiritualities. Then, about the middle of the twentieth century, Catholics at large began to feel a need for a more specifically "lay spirituality," because the spiritual ideals and practices being passed on to them from monastic communities were ill-suited to their life-situation in the world. So another kind of spirituality was developed.

Today, Roman Catholics and Christians at large use the term *spirituality* in a broader context, to mean anyone's lived relationship to Mystery. When that is further specified, as in New Age spirituality, Native American spirituality, Buddhist spirituality, we have a family of spiritualities, differing according to the way they understand and organize the spiritual life.

We have looked at how spirituality gives rise to religion. What does organized religion have to offer the spiritual pilgrim? First, it is community, and that means vital support on a long and daunting journey. Then religion has rituals, symbols, sacred texts, holy places. It has theologies, holy exemplars, educated leaders. In short, it has a lot of experience and a wealth of means. Even at that, it can always be further enriched, and it stands ever in need of reform and renewal. Organized religion generally constitutes spirituality's matrix of nurturance, a stable framework for its support. But spirituality remains religion's vital core. It challenges, expands, and reforms organized religion. The relationship is reciprocal, dynamic, mutually enriching.

Spiritual Insights, Spiritual Practices, and Complete Spiritualities

Some of the insights and practices which go under the name of spirituality today are mere bits and pieces, sometimes taken from an existing spiritual tradition, sometimes created afresh. Transcendental meditation, which came to the West in the '60s, is an import from Hinduism and Buddhism. It has value just in itself, for personal centering and quiet, whatever one's religious persuasions may be. The same can be said of the use of hypnosis and guided visualization to draw on the powers of the unconscious for physical healing, healing of memories, or general life direction. These are psychological discoveries, traceable to such seminal thinkers as Carl Jung and Roberto Assagioli. They have no direct link with religion. But it can generally be said that whatever enhances the life of the individual and the community is, from a Christian perspective, of God and according to God's purpose. For God's purpose is fullness of life for all. It can also be said that the psychological and the spiritual are hard to separate, for God dwells in all things and works in all things to realize the divine purpose. So, for example, dreams, which are psychologically viewed as the products of the unconscious, are biblically viewed as avenues of divine communication.

So there exist among us an abundance of spiritual insights and practices that are just bits and pieces, often with a life of their own. They are useful as far as they go. And then there are complete spiritualities. The major religions of the world are complete spiritualities. They teach not just a specific practice, but a whole way of life. They are of long standing, rich in all the elements elaborated at the end of the last section, and, by reason of their accumulated experience, tried and true.

A complete spirituality gives us three crucial possessions that a spiritual element, or even a cluster of them, usually do not: (1) an answer to the question of life's meaning; (2) a relationship with Mystery; and (3) a challenge to personal transformation. Each deserves some elaboration.

1. *An answer to the question of life's meaning.* We seek meaning in life, basic meaning. Especially in the face of all life's toil, its disappointments, its brokenness, we crave some sense of what it is really all about, of what might make it worthwhile even when it does not seem worthwhile, of how we are to orient ourselves amidst its pain and confusion.

What Is "Spirituality"?

From his years as a prisoner in Auschwitz, psychologist Viktor Frankl writes us a book about the crucial difference he notes between prisoners who survive the dreadful conditions of camp life and those who do not. The survivors have some driving meaning that keeps them going. Those who lack such purpose succumb to the forces of death. Out of this insight Frankl creates a new school of psychotherapy, logotherapy or meaning-therapy. In his view, it is not just the person in a concentration camp, nor just the person who seeks therapy, but each of us, whatever our circumstances, who has a profound need to find meaning in our life. Frankl states:

> According to logotherapy, the striving to find a meaning in one's life is the primary motivational force in man *[sic]*. That is why I speak of a *will to meaning* in contrast to the pleasure principle (or, as we could also term it, *the will to pleasure*) on which Freudian psychoanalysis is centered, as well as in contrast to the *will to power* stressed by Adlerian psychology.

A complete spirituality gives us an orientation in life—a set of values to live by, a sense of direction, and a basis for hope. We need that all the time. We need it even more if we are disabled, have just lost our best friend, or are watching old age strip us of status, home, and health. A man who lives each day in fear of sudden death from a heart condition offers us this insight into a deep human need:

> If I could be absolutely, positively, 100% sure that at the moment of death God does exist, and that I do have a soul, and that life after death and heaven await, this total peace of mind would be the greatest gift I can imagine.

2. A relationship with the Mystery. Because this seems so important to me, I want to reflect on it more at length.

Karl Rahner, in the course of some thirty or forty volumes of his abstruse "theological reflections," remarks several times quite simply, "God is our salvation." It leaps forth like a lightning bolt. Such a simple idea, yet so profound. If we have God, we have what we long for. We are "saved" in that sense. If we do not, we are empty, disoriented, wandering the world hungry.

The Psalms, those ancient prayers from centuries of Hebrew (human) experience, are filled with this theme.

> How much longer will you forget me, Yahweh? Forever?
> How much longer will you hide your face from me?
> How much longer must I endure grief in my soul
> and sorrow in my heart by day and by night? (Ps 13)

> O God, you are my God whom I eagerly seek;
> for you my flesh longs and my soul thirsts
> like the earth, parched, lifeless, and without water.
> For your love is better than life. (Ps 63)

When we read this inspired poetry, our hearts know exactly what it means. As St. Augustine remarked back in the fifth century, "You have made us for yourself, O Lord, and our hearts are restless until they rest in you."

Recently I was feeling depressed. It had hung around for some days, and I could not put my finger on what it was that was weighing me down. Finally I took time out and just sat with it. "What is all this?" I asked myself. At first, nothing came. I had to stay with it awhile before it spoke, but then suddenly there was the answer. It had two parts. First, I was struggling again against the conditions of existence—against things like the passage of time, the limits of my accomplishments, the work which, it seems, is never done, and all the hassles of life that intrude upon my peace. Sometimes I am pretty good about accepting the conditions of existence. On that day I realized that I was bucking them again, and making myself miserable in the process.

The second part of what came was that I was hungry for God. There it was, undeniable, strong, gnawing away inside. Already I felt better. I knew what I had to do. I made the choice to accept again the conditions of existence, a small price to pay for the privilege of existence. And I opened myself to God. "I want you, God," I said simply. And there God was, where I was. No vision. No message. But there God was, at the other end of my beam of longing—the Mystery, the Silence. I had not been spending enough time with that Presence. Life is livable without it. But when I go too long, I start to feel the deprivation.

Those of us who have been enriched by the writings of C. S. Lewis may not realize that he arrived at faith only after a years-long arduous trek. His was a cerebral quest. He read and read, and pondered and ruminated. Finally one night in his room, after going over in his mind for the umpteenth time all the arguments both for and against the existence of God, again unable to reach a conclusion, he knew he had to do something different. He tells us that he felt almost forced to his knees. Finally he opened his heart to the God he was seeking. He prayed. And there God was. Later, reflecting on all this, Lewis makes a trenchant observation about the simple longing for God, which had been at the center of his life for so many years. He says that our longing for God has more joy in it than most of life's consummations.

> True, it was desire and not possession. But then what I had felt on the walk had also been desire, and only possession in so far as that kind of desire is itself desirable, is the

fullest possession we can know on earth; or rather, because the very nature of Joy makes nonsense of our common distinction between having and wanting. There, to have is to want and to want is to have. Thus, the very moment when I longed to be so stabbed again, was itself again such a stabbing.

G. K. Chesterton, British essayist and Christian apologist who was very influential in C. S. Lewis's conversion, once remarked that there are only two things that satisfy the soul: a person and a story. Then he adds that even a story has to be about a person.

I do not know what the Buddhist feels when he sits in his silence. He does not believe in God, but sits there to be in contact with *something* at a very deep level. I suspect he feels the same peace I do. I think I am with *Someone*; he does not. To me that seems a huge difference.[9] I do not care to say the Buddhist is wrong and I am right. I do not want to convert him. I respect him as he is, and have not the slightest fear for his salvation. But in my own quest, I cannot be satisfied until I have found something like myself—something which, let us say by way of broad description, thinks, feels, chooses, expresses self, acts. I long for something which knows me and with which I can communicate, which is in that sense *Someone*, even if it be formless, unfathomable, and very, very quiet most of the time.

Two women who answered my questionnaire express this same hunger for God:

> I experience the longing for God, for union with God, every day—in the car, in the midst of grief, in the joy of being with my niece and nephew. For me, God is an experience of love, peace, joy.

> After the shock of my marital breakup, I had no desire to live. Everything lost its flavor. Now three and a half years later, I am leading a very full life—happy, busy, with no regrets. But however much I enjoy all the things I do, the attractions of the earth, even the love of my wonderful children, I am ready and even eager to go when God calls me home.

Some contemporary Western spiritual movements share with Buddhism an indifference to the question of God. Interest focuses simply on the expansion and improvement of the personality. This is fine as far as it goes. But it seems to me that if we lose a personal God, we lose big. While I have the greatest respect for the universe, with all its beauty and majesty, if you tell me it is less personal than I am, I am suddenly very lonely in a purely material ambience. All the blood goes out of it at once, the very Soul. I have enjoyed some great human loves. But if human companionship is the highest thing I can aspire to, I confess myself still hungry. And what about all the people who have never known a great human love, whose lives have, in fact, been starved for love? If whatever is ultimate or primary in the universe is not personal, then this profound human hunger for a great love is simply absurd. Then, as atheistic philosopher Jean-Paul Sartre said so well, each of us is just "a vain passion," doomed to lifelong frustration.

The hunger of which I speak is not a proof for a personal God. But it seems a strong hint. And I want briefly to mention two other such hints before closing this section. If whatever stands at the source of the evolution of the cosmos is not personal, then we have another anomaly. The universe shows such astonishing patterns of mind; how can it come from what is mindless? Human science works. Philosophy works. Mathematics works. All of them track the patterns of the universe. Why are there patterns at all? If there is no Mind, why are there such conspicuous evidences of design for the human mind to discover?

And a final conundrum. How can what is less than me, what lacks personality, have fashioned a being like *me*, who can feel, create, reflect, make choices, give myself in love? Am I, without any explanation, somehow incomparably greater than the blind forces that produced me?

This, then, is the second great deliverance of a complete spirituality: an I-Thou relationship with the Mystery. It meets a profound need of the human soul.

3. *A challenge to personal transformation.* A complete spirituality also stretches us. It makes demands. It stops us in our tracks sometimes. It catches us in our backsliding. We need that.

Look at the world. Take stock of the racism, sexism, homophobia. Contemplate the addictions. Consider the distribution of the goods of the earth. Look at the greed, the classes, the oppressions, the wars, the refugees, the hunger. Remember the state of earth itself. Something is wrong. Is a woman safe in the streets of the city? Is a child? What is going on in our homes? Is there harmony and contentment, an atmosphere that promotes the well-being and growth of each person? What do we find in our own hearts? Peace, a sense of purpose, and a surplus of love for all we meet? It is pretty clear that we could all use an injection of something, an inspiriting, and we need it over and over again. This is one of spirituality's main functions. It knows and names the vices. And it knows their remedies. It has a vision for personal growth and fulfillment, and a vision for the whole world. It reminds, goads, and empowers. A spirituality whose chief concern and lived manifestation is not ethical is a dubious spirituality indeed.

Let us, for the sake of comparison and contrast both with

assorted spiritual fragments and with other complete spiritualities, end this chapter by reviewing the main features of the spirituality most of us were suckled on. Grant that it has often been
presented less than compellingly, and lived less than inspiringly,
it remains a stirring vision, worthy of a total life commitment.

Grounded in a personal relationship with God, Christian
spirituality is life in the Spirit—by which is meant the Breath of
God, the Breath of Jesus. This foundational relationship affects
all one's other relationships and one's whole vision of the world.

Christian spirituality is lived in a community of persons called
the church, which gathers again and again for its nourishment
and direction around God's word and sacraments. This community is ordered to the gradual transformation of its members into
the fullness of their personhood as that is understood on the
model of Jesus. In addition to that, Christians have a mission to
the world—to help transform it into the reign of God. This dedication too is rooted in the activity and teaching of Jesus. The
reign of God, which Jesus labored to establish in the world and
on whose behalf he calls for collaborators, is built on justice,
love, peace, freedom, and celebration. The reign of God, Jesus'
grand dream, requires a total transformation of reality as we
know it. It begins in this world, and carries over into the next.[10]

Christian spirituality pushes us past mere surviving, past
ennui, past the pursuit of personal comfort, past the love of
family and tribe alone. It urges us toward our deepest possibilities of hoping, loving, and creating. It engenders a reverence
and concern for all persons, with a special care for the weak.
For this reason it also espouses the cause of earth. It cannot
rest until there is justice and fullness of life for all.

A woman in her fifties, answering the question, "What do you
seek spiritually at this time in your life?" manages in a personal
way to articulate the essentials of the Christian orientation:

I seek a spirituality that integrates my life. I seek communion with God but I want it to be the resource that moves
me to be with others in a way that speaks truth without
judging, encourages, accepts others as they are, expresses
compassion, provides hospitality for others to find themselves. I seek to know myself and to increase my ability to
both accept myself and to challenge myself. I want to live
with a sense of gratitude. My growing edge is extending
my love to the earth and to people I don't know. And I will
know this in the *actions* I take, not just attitude.

This is what it means to breathe the Breath of God.

Questions and Exercises

1. How do you define spirituality for yourself?

2. What difference, if any, does it make to you whether or
not a personal God is included in your pursuit of spirituality?

3. Slowly move through the Brussats' alphabet of spiritual
elements, reflecting on your own life in that regard. What
thoughts or feelings arise in you?

4. Recall two movies you have seen recently. Where do you
see spirituality operative in the lives of the main characters?

5. Choose a person as spiritually different from yourself as
you can find. Ask them about their spiritual life, and, in a dialogue in which you compare and contrast with mutual respect,
see what you can learn.

Chapter Four

How Can I Tell If I Am Making Progress in the Spiritual Life?

So passionate was Mullah Nasruddin's love for truth that he traveled to distant places in search of Koranic scholars, and he felt no inhibitions about drawing infidels at the bazaar into discussions about the truths of his faith.

One day his wife told him how unfairly he was treating her—and discovered that her husband had no interest whatsoever in that kind of truth.

—*Anthony de Mello, S.J.*

We are on a spiritual journey. How do we know we are on the right track? We seek to grow in the spiritual life. How do we know if we are making progress? Let me begin with a bit of personal history.

When I was in Catholic grade school and noontime came, we would all be marched in orderly lines down to the corner, and then be dismissed to go home for lunch. As we dispersed, I often ducked into the church for five minutes to make a visit.

57

This was not common practice, I couldn't help noticing. I was the only one there. But I think that is what I loved about it. There I was alone with the Alone, in the silence of the church. It was a place of great peace and consolation for me.

Meanwhile, back among the people outside sacred space, I had a habit of poking the girl who sat in front of me with a lead pencil. She never made an issue of it. But her mother did one night when she noticed pencil marks in her daughter's back and called up the teacher. There was, in addition, a boy I picked on, a kid smaller than myself, whom I would torment if I chanced upon him in unprotected places around school. Back home, I was rejecting the sibling who needed me the most. She pleased me not, and I simply ignored her, leaving her to flounder in her lonely world. What do you think of my spirituality?

Spirituality is tricky. In this chapter, let us see if we can establish some criteria for discerning both genuine spirituality and true spiritual growth. First, let us consider some reliable signs of spiritual progress. Then, let us take up the question of incorporation or grafting. Many people who stand within the Christian tradition today feel an attraction to elements of other traditions. How can we tell whether ideas and practices from other traditions will help the cause or hurt it? Finally, let us look at some of the common temptations we are likely to encounter on a spiritual course, considering pitfalls both to groups and to ourselves as individuals.

Signs of Spiritual Progress

How do we know whether or not we are growing in the spiritual life?

In 1968, a mixed group of Zen Buddhist and Christian monks gathered in Kyoto for several days of prayer and dialogue. They made a discovery that similar groups have made since. When they sat together in meditation, they felt at one with one another in the silence. When they talked at meals, they enjoyed and felt respect for one another as genuinely spiritual persons. When they spoke of values, they agreed easily on what was important in life and what constituted a good person. When they tried to formulate theological principles or religious dogmas, they could not agree on a single one.[1]

It is this last area that makes for the differences among the religions—philosophical propositions, the attempt to map ultimate reality. Little wonder. This is the realm of Mystery. Whether the Ultimate is one or many, personal or impersonal, unitarian or trinitarian, properly called Allah, Yahweh, Great Spirit, Brahman, or God; whether there is life after death, and how that is best described; of what components the human person is made up; which historical individual is the most perfect incarnation of the divine—religious thinkers have always differed on these profound questions and probably always will. This is not such a problem. What is a problem *is* that wars have been fought over particular beliefs about these matters, and countless human beings killed, or at least cruelly persecuted.

When, on the other hand, attention is focused on spiritual *values* rather than dogmas, consensus comes quickly, as the Kyoto experience attests. Those who are influenced by the same Spirit quickly recognize one another, though they belong to different religious groups. What are these values around which all spiritual persons unite?

Let us examine the list already most familiar to us. In his letter to the Galatians, St. Paul writes of what he calls "the fruits of the Spirit." He sets them in contrast to what he calls "the works of the flesh." When Paul says "flesh," he does not mean the body, so he is not saying the soul is good, the body and all material things bad. It is evident from his list of "works of the flesh" that several of them have nothing to do with the body at all. By "flesh" Paul means the tendency toward evil that is present in our total being. By "spirit" he means the tendency toward good that is present in our total being. Here are his contrasting sets of "fruits":

> Now the works of the flesh are plain: fornication, impurity, licentiousness, idolatry, sorcery, enmity, strife, jealousy, anger, selfishness, dissension, party spirit, envy, drunkenness, carousing, and the like....But the fruit of the Spirit is love, joy, peace, patience, kindness, goodness, faithfulness, gentleness, self-control. (Gal 5:19-23)

It is difficult to imagine a spiritual person in any tradition who would argue against any of Paul's fruits of the spirit. It is plain that love, peace, kindness, self-control, and such are genuinely spiritual and admirable qualities in any person. In fact, Paul's short list could be filled out, and people of every spiritual tradition would agree that living these values is the spiritual life. For all the great traditions already speak of them, including Paul's: *truthfulness, hopefulness, acceptance of self and others, compassion, nonviolence, generosity, forgiveness, simplicity of life, prayerfulness, humility.* Who will quarrel? Even those who would not identify themselves as spiritual would doubtless say they admire people who exhibit such traits, and deep down would like to be this kind of person themselves.

So how do I know I am on the right track? How can I tell if I am making spiritual progress? Well, am I becoming more hopeful, more serene? Simpler in my lifestyle? More generous toward others? More accepting of others? Readier to forgive those who wrong me? Am I doing something on the larger scale to relieve human suffering and make life better for others? Am I growing in my groundedness in God, my Higher Power, or whatever I call that from which I live? Less controlling, more trusting? When we put the emphasis on the values and virtues we need to cultivate, we can see how difficult the spiritual journey is. It takes a lifetime. We are always on the way. It all has to do with what kind of person we want to become, what kind of life we want to be living.

If we dedicate ourselves to life in the spirit, a transformation takes place in us, but only very gradually. Not for nothing do Buddhist monks sit for years facing the wall. A transformation *has* to take place in us. Without it, we remain anxious, mean-spirited, narrow-minded, intolerant, self-absorbed, caught up in petty pursuits, shackled by our addictions, a burden to ourselves, hurtful toward others and the earth. We leave the world a worse place than we found it. Would that the spiritual life were as pleasant and life-enhancing a pursuit as some gurus today would have us believe—simply a matter of making more time for ourselves and our hobbies, keeping our bodies functioning well by healthy self-talk, making more money by cultivating a positive attitude and aligning ourselves with the energies of the universe, enlarging our circle of friends by keeping a smile on our face and showing good energy. No, a genuinely spiritual life keeps calling for a change of heart. And the heart, we find, does not so easily change.

Near the end of his public life, Jesus puts his chief criterion of genuine spirituality into a parable of a final judgment scene at the end of the world (Mt 25:31–46). His ultimate spiritual standard is this: What kind of response did you make when you saw people in need? For Jesus, the litmus test of spirituality is always love: love of self, love of God, love of others. Now, we all love sometimes. But love as a way of life remains quite a challenge,

61

whether in the marketplace or at home. It is an ideal calling us again and again to growth.

Incorporating Elements from Other Traditions

In our contemporary situation, all the great religious traditions and several new ones live in our very neighborhood and admit of easy access. No need to travel to India or Thailand to encounter Hinduism or Buddhism, or to Saudi Arabia to shake hands with Islam. Their books are in our bookstores, their practitioners down the street.

Even without our seeking it out personally, there is already cross-fertilization among spiritual traditions. Gandhi's nonviolent approach to social change is well known and in wide use now by Christian activists. Native American attitudes toward the earth have been assimilated into Christian spirituality. Buddhist methods of meditation are fairly widely used by Christians. Goddess religions, under feminist exploration, have yielded fresh images of the Mystery, which many within our churches have found fruitful.

Are there any criteria by which we can decide what is good or bad here, what is helpful or what might be harmful?

First, let us consider the matter of one's basic stance. It is one thing to stand within a religious tradition, and discerningly incorporate into it elements from other traditions. It is quite another to throw one's tradition away and stand nowhere, and then try to piece together a new spirituality out of a bit of this and a bit of that. In the first case, one already has a worldview and an approach to life, and is modifying and enriching them. One possesses something tried and true and is endeavoring to make it even better. In the second case, one is starting from scratch, without even a principle of discernment. One is vintage pioneer, charging into the forest without a map. But is that the best way to go? This book is written from the premise that those of us who were raised in the Christian tradition do best to stay within it despite its problems, to refurbish its own best possessions, and to incorporate into it whatever else of value we might find. University of Chicago's Martin Marty, renowned historian of religion, is fond of putting it this way: Keep one foot inside the tradition, and let the other foot wander.[2]

To return, then, to the spiritual elements catalogued above, it is obvious almost from the mere naming of them that they are good and helpful. Gandhi's nonviolent resistance to evil is perfectly consistent with the spirit and practice of Jesus. Gandhi was, in fact, inspired by Jesus, and his historic movement caused Christians to reread the New Testament and dust off their own forgotten nonviolent heritage and history of conscientious objection. Feminist theology has already immensely enriched the church in thought and practice, and will continue to. The Native American tradition has not only heightened public awareness to our ecological peril, but has stimulated Christians to dig into their own sources for testimonies to earth's sacredness. And we have found them.

It is probably in the matter of prayer and worship, where we deal so immediately with the Sacred, that we most wonder what is consistent or inconsistent with what we have learned and lived. Is Buddhist meditation acceptable as Christian prayer? Are Christians on safe ground in creating their own sacred rituals? Can we pray to Goddess as well as God?

St. Ignatius laid down a very helpful principle in his *Spiritual Exercises* for all one's choices in the spiritual life: Use what conduces to the goal, and avoid what does not. The goal is union with God. Ignatius was quite free as to particular means. In prayer, what we seek is to be in communion with the Mystery. The Mystery is always present to us. The problem is that we are usually not present to the Mystery. Whatever methods or means help us to find that space where we can be quietly together are all to the good, whoever proposes it. Someone might object that Christian prayer is supposed to be Christ-centered, and Buddhist meditation methods know nothing of Christ. But as Christians, we know that we are already in Christ; and that Jesus pointed much more consistently to the God he believed in than to himself as the object of our prayer and worship—the God to whom he himself prayed.

When in the 1960s young Americans began traveling to India to learn Eastern methods of meditation, Christian leaders were propelled into making available to the whole church the riches of our own contemplative tradition, then the preserve of monastic groups. The method which has achieved the widest dissemination is what is called Centering Prayer, which takes its origin from the Jesus Prayer of the early Christian centuries.[3] Centering prayer is very simple. It entertains no image or concept for God, and uses no words to communicate. It employs only a mantric sort of pointer to keep one's attention focused on the Silence. This is very similar to common Buddhist methods of meditation, only the faith-context differing in which the person meditating is situated. Jesuit Father Anthony de Mello, born in India, where he also spent his entire working life, proposes a great variety of approaches to prayer in his book *Sadhana*, written for Christians.[4] An experienced spiritual guide, he draws on his familiarity with several of the world's spiritual traditions. His prayer exercises range from merely focusing on one's breathing, to guided fantasy, to prayers of devotion. He comments on aspects of prayer regularly as he moves through these exercises.

Nothing he says implies that any of the methods are superior to any of the others. His entire approach to the subject is guided by the principle: Use what works for you. We find a similar attitude in Hindu scholar and Christian believer Diana Eck, who draws on several traditions in teaching what all experts on prayer regard as crucial: the attainment of silence and attentiveness. [5]

In communal rituals, again it is openness to the Sacred that is sought so that It might permeate more and more of our existence. Communion with the Sacred calls for quiet, reverence, and receptivity. Any of a great variety of symbols, readings, music, and symbolic actions can intensify the presence and action of the Sacred in our midst. We saw in an earlier chapter that the Sacred itself can be symbolized in myriad ways—masculine, feminine, or impersonal. There is no harm at all in creating our own rituals. Even to relatively fixed rituals of long standing, people are constantly bringing creativity lest they tail off into tedium. For some of our needs, no ritual exists, or what exists does not seem suitable. Jesus' pragmatic criterion is applicable to sacred rituals as well as to other spiritual practices: By their fruits you will know them (Mt 7:20). Watch for the sort of effects your ritual expressions have on your life.

An experienced spiritual guide constitutes another kind of touchstone or criterion where the spiritual life is concerned. Having a regular talk with such a person in which you lay out everything you are doing, ask questions and seek specific guidance has proved through the centuries to be an invaluable assist on the journey, not only for wisdom but for support.

In sum, other spiritual traditions have much to offer us. They have enriched the lives of countless millions before we stumbled on them. We can test any particular spiritual idea or practice by its fruits. We keep using what conduces to our goal of union with God and a life well lived. The rest we can let go.

Common Temptations of Spiritual Groups and Individuals

The spiritual life has its hazards. They are classically called temptations, and they occur quite freely both to groups and individuals. By temptations I mean attractions to beliefs or courses of action which, while they may seem at first sight to be good, actually pull us off the path of spiritual growth.

We have noted how spiritual seekers tend naturally to join together in groups small and large for leadership, support, and sharing. In our own day, we have seen some small religious groups come to grief. And a cursory acquaintance with history informs us that even the major religions have done great harm along with the good they have done. Aware of these dangers, representatives of most of the world's religions have met to try to establish criteria by which religious belief and practice can be measured, no matter whose they may be.

The criterion on which they have come to agree is *the human good, individual and collective.*[6] That is what spirituality is meant to promote. This is why it has been embraced and has always been part of human culture. It arises both from felt need and from discovery. It is developed to enhance the life of the individual and the whole community—to give life deeper meaning, to foster genuine personal development, and to strengthen the bonds of community. And so we can assert, and religious leaders have, that a religion or any religious element (doctrine, institution, practice, person) are authentic if they do actually promote the human good, individual and communal, and are inauthentic if they work against them. Jesus made this same point quite simply when he made persons primary over religious practice: "The sabbath was made for human beings, not human beings for the sabbath" (Mk 2:27).

With this criterion in mind, let us look more closely now at spiritual groups and their programs, sifting for authenticity.

Clearly to be called into question are groups that use thought control. They carefully keep out other points of view, dismiss them contemptuously, or attribute them to Satan. Not only do such groups oppress their own members. They promote division and enmity in the larger community by demonizing people who are different from them.

Skepticism is the appropriate response when an ideology presents a view of the world that reduces complex issues to simplistic either/or terms. Though life might be easier if reality were so simple, the fact is that truth is hard to pin down and, when found, often seen to be many-sided. Ask any person who has lived awhile. They know how difficult it is to make the ethical/spiritual call in common situations. God's favorite color in many important matters of life, it seems, is gray.

Be suspicious when a school of spirituality teaches that there is one way only—our way. There are far too many good people doing well on other paths for this to be true.

Be wary of leaders who insist on blind obedience, whether their appeal is to personal charism or divine warrant. It is never wise to surrender your own capacity to think critically, or you are wholly at the mercy of any claimant to expertise or authority. And trust your experience. Are the ideas proposed here as true confirmed by your experience?

Beware of leaders who live lavishly on the profits of their spiritual work. Is this spirituality? There are three items to watch closely if you want to assess the quality of spiritual life in a community: money, sex, and power. What is the community's money being spent on? Who is having sex with whom and what does it mean? And how is power being used? To develop this last point just a bit, is power used to control, coerce, and intimidate? Or is it used to serve and to empower others? Also, is there any significant power being exercised in the form of the persuasive power of a good example? That is how a good leader best leads. Think of Mother Teresa, Gandhi, Jesus. Where leadership is concerned, discern carefully: What kind of person is this? What kind of life does he or she live? What kind of person is attracted to this group, and what kind of lives are they living? "By their fruits you will know them," Jesus answered when asked how to distinguish the genuine article from the spurious in matters spiritual (Mt 7:20). His was the pragmatic test. A good tree bears good fruit, a bad tree bad.

Be cautious when your entrance into a group entails giving up everything you own, or revealing personal information that could be used against you, because it will be very difficult to leave if ever you want to.

So much for spiritual groupings. On the personal level, all of us need to be aware of certain false quests. There is the quest of religious experience or religious feelings. They are wonderful when they happen, a surprise gift; but they should never be the object of direct seeking. It is a little like wanting sex with someone instead of love. Another temptation is to fall for promises of quick salvation or instant enlightenment. We would all love it, and many purport to deliver it, but, alas, there is no such thing.

Be suspicious of feelings of righteousness, by which I mean the assurance of being right, holy, spiritual, saved, among the elect. Those who are genuinely spiritual or truly close to God never exhibit airs like these. They are convinced they are mere beginners at the spiritual life though they have been at it for seventy years, far more keenly sensible of what they have not attained than of what they have.

Be wary also of the quest of the magical—a way to pray that will surely get results, a laying on of hands that always works wonders, extraordinary powers of perception or discernment, clear signs from God, verbal messages (so often for other people). We would all love to have such access to the transcendent, but it is very rarely given. We live by faith most of the time, and make our choices by our best lights, which are not terribly bright. The glitter of religion and spirituality must always be distinguished from the gold, which lies deeper and is harder won.

The most common temptation of all, and probably the hardest to fight, is discouragement. It assails every spiritual pilgrim after the initial enthusiasm wears off and the journey settles down into the plains. Such a long trek, and so little to show after so much effort; perhaps I should just give it up. Classical spiritual writer William Faber used to call it "weariness in well-doing." Perfectionism is the enemy here: "If it isn't perfect, it isn't worth doing." But it is. Something is better than nothing, always. The spiritual journey *is* long. Dramatic breakthroughs are rare. Patience, perseverance, and humility carry the day.

In summary, there are a number of criteria by which we can measure spiritual communities, spiritual elements, and our own progress. They are:

- The pragmatic test: By their fruits you will know them
- Jesus' great commandment: Love of God, love of self, love of neighbor
- Paul's fruits of the spirit: charity, joy, peace, etc., and similar lists of virtues across the religious spectrum
- The judgment of an experienced spiritual guide
- The human good, individual and communal

Questions and Exercises

1. What is the relationship between spirituality and religion? How important is religion in your own spiritual quest?

2. Why do you suppose it is that organized religion, which exists to promote the spiritual life, also manages to do great harm? What harm are you aware of, done not only by other religions, but by your own?

3. There are many spiritual leaders, groups, and paths competing for your attention in today's spiritual marketplace. How do you decide what to buy and what to leave alone?

4. Using the criteria offered in this chapter, consider some spiritual beliefs or practices you are familiar with from such sources as Judaism, Native American spirituality, Buddhism, or New Age spirituality. Do you consider them to be helpful or harmful for Christians?

5. What are some signs by which we can recognize growth in the spiritual life? Would these be much the same across the spectrum of religions, or significantly different?

Chapter Five

Jesus: Trailblazer, Window to the Mystery

The figure of a Jesus of the poor, who defends their cause and takes up their lot, who enters the world's conflict and dies at the hands of the mighty, and who thus proclaims and is good news, is still fundamentally and eternally new. This is why I keep writing and publishing about Jesus.

—*Jon Sobrino, S.J.*

In flights of the spirit, as in other human adventures, there are many who would embark on the journey free as birds, innocent of all assumptions, unencumbered by any baggage, wanting to discover everything for themselves.

On the other hand, there lived a rabbi in first-century Israel, Yeshua by name, who left us a spiritual map. He was at the very least a notable spiritual pilgrim who made a profound impression on his contemporaries. Every age since has acknowledged him as estimable—original, profound, free. We are in possession of large parts of his legacy—the way of wisdom he taught and lived. Countless people have found inspiration in it.[1] To take a recent example, Mohandas Gandhi, one of the spiritual giants of the twentieth century, expressed the deepest admiration for Yeshua and acknowledged his indebtedness, making the sermon on the Mount his particular study.

Before we proceed too much further on our spiritual journey, we might do well to take another look at Yeshua (Jesus' original Aramaic name) to see what he may have to offer us. Let us look first at his life and teaching as the gospels present them, then at his death and resurrection. Finally, let us note some of the questions people are asking about Jesus today, and how theologians are answering them.[2]

Jesus' Life and Teaching

Perhaps the most unmistakable feature of the life of Jesus is the centrality and depth of his relationship with God. It shows in many ways. He prays much. We find him at prayer not only at critical junctures in his life—when he is baptized, when he chooses the Twelve, when he is in agony in the garden—but whenever he can get away from the crowds of a morning or evening (Mk 1:35). He speaks familiarly of God in parables and other teachings, as if he knows exactly how God sees things and what God wants of human beings. So assured is he of his teaching about God that people remark: "He teaches as one having authority, and not as the scribes and Pharisees" (Mt 7:29). Jesus conducts himself as a person on a mission, seeking always to do the will of the One who sent him, striving to accomplish God's work (Jn 4:34). He frequently refers to God as "my Father," not just as "our Father" (Jn 20:17), and goes further still, calling God "Abba" (Mk 14:36) a more familiar term like "Papa." This Father of Jesus is not the traditional patriarch, but One whose chief mark is compassion. In this God Jesus puts his trust, in life and in death.

Uniquely intimate as Jesus' relationship with God is, he describes that God as gracious to *all*, as wanting to relate in love with every person. Jesus teaches that we are all God's children, that God has numbered the hairs of our heads, that God will give us what we ask for, that in fact God knows what we need before we ask, and that God will take care of our needs if we seek to do what is right (Mt 6:33). Jesus teaches that we show our love for God by doing God's will (Mt 7:21). Yet, in his parables as well as in his own ministry, Jesus shows God's readiness to forgive us our failings and continue to be faithful to us in spite of them (Lk 15).

A second prominent feature of the life of Jesus is that he lives so much for others, and the cornerstone of his teaching is that we too must all have this kind of love for everyone. Open the gospel to any page, and you will find Jesus doing something for someone. He is forgiving sins, healing diseases, freeing people from what limits them, feeding a crowd, calming a storm, teaching or answering questions, inviting or encouraging someone. He boldly confronts religious and political leaders for the way they cause suffering to others (e.g., Mt 23). He feels others' pain and does all he can to ease it (Mt 9:36). Indeed his dedication to God seems to be expressed chiefly in this total commitment to the well-being of the human community.

There is something remarkable about the scope of his love. Most people love someone. It seems that Jesus had a heart large enough to embrace everyone. Though he was sought out by some of the rich and powerful of his day, his preference was for those at the bottom of the social ladder. He eats with prostitutes and "sinners" with sufficient regularity to get the reputation of being "a glutton and a drunkard, a friend of tax collectors and sinners" (Mt 11:19). He shows interest in and appreciation of women in a culture in which men generally looked down on women. He allows himself to be accosted in public by lepers and cripples, blind people, deaf people. In religious terms, Jesus is neither an ascetic nor a hermit. Rather, he is a person in the midst of the human community, helping people as best he can with the difficulties of life. He succeeds in reviving people's faith in themselves and moving them to relate to others as he does.

Jesus calls people to follow him. He urges them to share their goods with others (Mk 10), to help the person who has fallen victim at the side of the road (Lk 10), to feed the hungry and visit the prisoner (Mt 25). He asks them to forgive those who have injured them, and to do it over and over (Mt 18). He encourages them to love not just their friends but their enemies as well—those who hate them, speak ill of them, persecute them—and to do good to these people (Lk 6:27). He asks them to serve one another even to washing each other's feet (Jn 13), and to seek the lowest place rather than the highest (Lk 14). In Jesus' view, it is not enough to love just family and friends, or even just those of one's own nation or religion. His vision of community takes in all humanity. He seeks to break down all barriers that stand between "them" and "us," to reconcile all human beings with one another and with God. His spirituality is this-worldly and practical. It makes demands.

The teaching of Jesus is brought to focus in his own simple summary of it, given in Jerusalem near the end of his public life. He tells us what he means when he stresses doing God's will as the heart of the spiritual life. In answer to a question as to which of God's commandments is the greatest, he says:

> "The first is, 'Hear, O Israel, the Lord our God is one
> God, and you must love the Lord your God with your

whole heart and with your whole soul and with your whole mind and with your whole strength.' The second is this, 'You must love your neighbor as yourself.'" (Mk 12:30–31)

Jesus is quoting his people's scriptures, Deuteronomy 6:4–6 and Leviticus 19:18. The spiritual genius of Jesus consists precisely in the intertwining of the two parts of this one commandment. The quality of our relationships with fellow human beings is here made the chief indication of our seriousness about God. It was the chief expression of Jesus' own dedication. John later puts it this way:

> If you say, "I love God," and you hate your brother or sister, you are a liar; for if you do not love a brother or sister whom you have seen, you cannot love God whom you have not seen. (1 Jn 4:20)

There is another major emphasis in the teaching of Jesus, and it flows from the great commandment. In many different ways, he enjoins the renunciation of riches. He tells us not to lay up treasure for ourselves on earth (Mt 6). He calls the poor blessed, and pronounces woes on the rich (Lk 6). He tells a rich young man to sell everything he has and give to the poor, and come and follow him (Mk 10). He says it is easier for a camel to get through the eye of a needle than for a rich person to enter God's kingdom (Mk 10). In a parable, he describes a man who is busy building himself bigger barns, and calls him a fool (Lk 12). His parable of the rich man and the beggar at his gate ends with the beggar in the bosom of Abraham and the rich man in Hades (Lk 16). The way this theme in Jesus' teaching flows from the overarching commandment is, first, as he says himself, we cannot serve both God and mammon (Mt 7:24). They represent conflicting sets of values. Second, there are so many needy people around us that we can hardly say we love them when we are busy building ourselves an economic empire and walling them out. If today's world were a "global village" of one thousand people, sixty persons would have half the income, five hundred would be hungry, six hundred would live in shantytowns, and seven hundred would be illiterate.[3] In such a world, the emphasis Jesus lays on economics still has bite.

Before we leave the teaching of Jesus, we might make reference to one item absent from our summary. That is sex. The reason sex is not here is that it is at best a minor key in the life and teaching of Jesus. This seems worth remarking because so often when the Christian life is presented, sexual prohibitions are a very prominent part of the presentation. Indeed, the image of the Christian church in many minds is that of an institution negatively preoccupied with sex.

If Jesus had shown a negative attitude toward sexuality and made sex a big issue, the church's stance would be understandable. But sex is a subject on which Jesus says very little. There is nothing in the gospels on masturbation, homosexuality, premarital sex, or birth control. Jesus does speak against adultery, but adultery involves a serious breach of marital covenant. He speaks against lust, but this teaching is found in only one of the four gospels, where it takes up just one verse (Mt 5:28). Nowhere in the New Testament are we told Jesus was celibate. If he was, he makes no point of it, and the men in his inner circle of disciples are all married, with the possible exception of John. When Jesus deals with anyone who has gone wrong sexually, he simply forgives the person, no questions asked. The gospels hardly constitute a basis for the church's preoccupation with sexual issues. Paul's letters lie at the root of some of it, along with dualistic (spirit vs. body) non-Christian cultural currents that insinuated themselves into early Christian theology.

This is not to say sexuality is not an important moral/spiritual issue. It is, obviously, and we will have more to say about it in chapter 8. Sexual exploitation hurts people. Integrating our sexual energy into authentic and responsible loving is for everyone a personal task at once crucial and sufficiently challenging to last a lifetime. Jesus gives us the *norm* for the expression of our sexuality—a love that is true—but he offers no detailed sexual ethic. And it is unmistakable that when he talks about love, he talks ten times more about its economic implications than he does about its sexual implications. The churches, for whatever reasons, have exactly reversed the proportions.

Jesus' Death

We can hardly speak of the life of Jesus without talking about his death, not only because he is famous for the way he died, but also because the manner of it flowed quite predictably from his life. It should not surprise us that Jesus did not live to be very old. The end came violently, as it was almost bound to. It has sometimes been said that his crucifixion was the whole purpose of his existence, that "he came down to die." This is far too simple. Whatever good God may have been able to bring out of Jesus' suffering and death, the tragedy of his execution has as plain a this-worldly causality as other such events do. It was precisely the things Jesus said and did that turned the authorities against him and generated their resolve to destroy him.

There is a perfect parallel here with the life stories of such people as Mohandas Gandhi and Martin Luther King, Jr. Jesus challenged the established order, and the powerful saw to his removal from the scene. He did not cultivate the society of the rich and powerful, though he would doubtless have found welcome among them had he embraced their values. He did not abide by the accepted social and religious norms of his day. He set aside sabbath observance when he saw someone in need (Mk 3:1), and fasting laws when he saw greater good in eating and drinking with people. At meals he did not always observe the proprieties of ritual purification (Mk 7). He challenged the reigning religious authorities for legalistically laying burdens on people and not lifting a finger to help, for consuming the substance of widows, for fasting and giving alms in public places mainly to be seen, for preferring strict observance in tiny matters of law to the larger demands of justice, mercy, and faith (Mt 23). He accused them also of killing the prophets God had sent them time and again to call them to conversion. In a symbolic gesture, he cut them to the quick by making public protest against the commerce going on in the temple (Mk 12). He embarrassed them further with his outrageous demand that the rich give up their surplus to relieve the sufferings of the poor. Like that of other prophets before and after him, Jesus' theology was political.

He attracted a great following. Just as he was offensive to those in power, he was very popular with those who were not. In him they saw the possibility of their liberation, and wanted to make him king (Jn 6:15). Jesus never accepted these offers, but he had come to pose such a threat to the status quo that both Jewish and Roman authorities were well aware of him and very uneasy about him. In combination, they resolved to do away with him on criminal charges. They managed to get him arrested and brought to trial, where they alleged that he was stirring up the people, opposing the tribute to Caesar, and making himself a king (Lk 23:2). The Roman governor Pilate could not find criminal cause in any of this, but gave way to pressure and had Jesus publicly flogged and executed (Lk 23:13). And so Jesus met his fate, crucified between two thieves.

It is chiefly liberation theology, a fresh approach to theological reflection originating in Latin America in the last several decades, which has opened our eyes to the intrinsic connection between Jesus' life and his crucifixion: that his death has this-worldly causes, that it is, in fact, the logical outcome of the sorts of things he was saying and doing.[4] Prior to this insight, Jesus' life, teaching, and example were usually seen as having their own value and taught accordingly, while his death was viewed as having quite a distinct purpose, designed not on earth but in heaven: to make satisfaction to God for the sins of the world.

Jesus' Resurrection

The resurrection of Jesus may seem to lie outside the pale of historical verifiability, but it is such an essential part of the story of Jesus that we can scarcely pass over it in silence. Jesus' death was felt as a great tragedy by those who followed him. It seemed it was all over, period, and what an ending. Many feared for their own lives and scattered as he fell. Some stayed huddled together in desolation and fear, all their hopes dashed. It is against this bleak horizon that the resurrection dawns. Jesus is seen alive. At first his disciples are incredulous, but their unbelief slowly turns to belief as witness after witness comes in.

The gospel accounts of Jesus' appearances describe several scenes in which he comes unexpectedly on a situation of discouragement and turns it into a celebration—on the women leaving the empty tomb (Mt 28), on Mary weeping at the tomb (Jn 20), on the disciples huddled in the upper room (Lk 24), on the two walking dejectedly back to Emmaus (Lk 24), on the disciples returning to their fishing and coming up empty (Jn 21). In his

First Letter to the Corinthians, Paul makes a list of people who saw the risen Jesus—Peter, the Twelve, a group of five hundred, James, all the apostles, and finally himself, Paul, a man looking the other way (1 Cor 15:3–8).

Since none of us has ever experienced the resurrection of anyone from the dead, we might be disinclined to put any credence in these testimonies of an ancient people. This skepticism, reasonable as it is, has to contend with one rather massive fact. In the face of persecution and against great odds, Christianity rapidly became the dominant religion of the Roman Empire. It is hard to imagine people going to their deaths by burning, crucifixion, wild beasts, or beheading, stoutly holding out for a resurrection they just imagined and dearly wished to be true. It is hard to imagine their taking this individual and his teachings seriously enough to build a literature and a movement around him when the legitimate religious authorities of a very religious society condemned him as a blasphemer and troublemaker and called for his crucifixion. If Jesus had never been heard from after his death, we might have some written recollections of a remarkable historical figure, but it seems most unlikely that we would have the church.

There are aspects of the death and resurrection of Jesus that would make almost any spiritual pilgrim think. His willingness to undergo a painful death as a consequence of what he was saying and doing, neither backing down nor fleeing when he saw what was shaping up, attests to his strong conviction of the rightness of his life's dedication and his deep trust in the God in whom he placed his hope. That God raised him from death and showed him to those who had followed him validates all that he stood for. This is the more remarkable when it is realized that Jesus was religiously unorthodox. His claims about how God wanted to be served appalled the religious leaders of his day and divided the general populace. He revised the way his people thought about their scriptures. He laid claim to a significant role in God's plan for human history. He insisted that God is loving, faithful, and merciful. He underscored God's concern for all who are oppressed by others and God's desire that there be justice and fullness of life for all. All of this was called into question when he was crucified by the religious and political leaders of his society as a dangerous person. Had there been no resurrection, we would be left wondering if Jesus was not deceived in his fundamental convictions.

Also important for spirituality is the paradigmatic nature of Jesus' death and resurrection. It illumines the riddle of human existence. What is most baffling about our life is all the suffering we undergo—the toil, the frustration, the injustice, the struggle, the losses. So heavy is all this at times that life seems joyless, hopeless. The death and resurrection of Jesus helps us understand the puzzle of suffering and death and gives us a basis for hope. Perhaps for us too, suffering and dying are not final, but are a passage to some kind of new life. In this climactic moment of his career, Jesus demonstrates in action what he had previously proclaimed as the core paradox:

> Unless the grain of wheat falls into the ground and dies, it remains just a grain; but if it dies, it bears much fruit. (Jn 12:24)

And in another place:

> Those who want to save their lives will lose them; but those who lose their lives for my sake and the sake of the gospel will save them. (Mk 8:35)

Many times Jesus employs seed parables to get across this crucial concept (e.g., Mk 13). All of them depict a planting that results in the death of seeds as they were and the bursting forth of something greater. Then he dramatizes it in his own death and resurrection, which thus becomes the cardinal Christian paradigm. It reveals that God works within the mystery of our suffering to bring good out of evil, meaning out of absurdity, life out of death.

Jesus and the Mystery

It seems evident that Jesus has much to offer the person seeking spiritual life. His teaching is at once inspiring and profoundly challenging, and one hears in it not only a call to personal growth but principles for the solution of problems afflicting the human community. But there is more than a teaching here. There is the power of a life beautifully lived. Jesus still lives in the gospels, a figure attractive, inspiring, compelling.

Running through Jesus' entire career as its central theme is his testimony about what we have called the Mystery, or the deepest dimension of all reality. Since it is *that* which spiritual persons wish to contact and be in harmonious and empowered relationship with, we might linger one final moment to recall what Jesus had to say about it.

This man, whom the New Testament calls "trustworthy witness" (Rev 1:5) attests that the Mystery is personal, benevolent, and interested in us. What an immense difference this simple declaration makes to our view of the universe and of ourselves. It changes everything, answering the most important question of all. The Mystery wants a friendly relationship with us, which is precisely what we also most deeply want.

Jesus teaches and models the way of life that brings us into the deepest harmony with the Mystery.

American theologian Michael Buckley, in a book on atheism, sets forth the arresting thesis that in its attempt to respond to contemporary atheism, Christian theology has made a big mistake. It has tried to establish the reality of God solely from nature, creating proofs for God from the workings of the cosmos, forgetting all about the witness of Jesus.[5] It is true that nature bears God's signature. But what about the compelling testimony of Yeshua, at the very least a mystic and a prophet? He stands on what he has known and experienced personally; he stakes his whole life on it. If there is no God, or if *God* is just another word for impersonal cosmic energies, then Yeshua is simply absurd. But can he be? Is there any way we can reduce him to a mere idealist and a dreamer, or a man mentally ill? Read the gospels and see if that is the conclusion that makes the best sense to you.

What Is the Relationship between Jesus and God?

Spiritual pilgrims from many backgrounds are asking questions today about Jesus, as they attempt to figure out how he fits into their life journeys. They are attracted to him, yet run up against difficulties. The questions and assertions I hear most frequently as a theology professor and spiritual guide revolve around the claim that Jesus is God and the idea that he died for our sins.

- *If Jesus is God, he is difficult to relate to as a model for us.* What is the point in talking about his immense generosity in life, his courage in facing death, or the depth of his prayer life?

His experience is simply not our experience, his life not our life. We can admire him, but we cannot identify with him. His heroism is not a genuinely human heroism but the heroism of a superbeing. We can appreciate his life as a story of how God was willing to reduce self to the stature of a mere human being and experience human life. But if Jesus is God, he is not really one of us, even if you say he is also somehow human.

- *If Jesus is God, Christianity is clearly the one true religion.* Every other religion's founder is a mere human being. So Christianity is truth right from the mouth of God, housed in an institution founded by God. The other religions are all mere human gropings. The dialogue of the religions becomes ridiculous. What could anybody else possibly teach Christians? It is also sometimes claimed that people are eternally lost unless they embrace God's one true religion. But these positions run up against immense difficulties.

The actual religious situation of humanity today, as summarized by the World Development Forum, is this. If our "global village" were a community of a thousand people, there would be:

329	Christians
174	Muslims
131	Hindus
61	Buddhists
52	Animists
3	Jews
34	Members of other religions (e.g., Sikhs, Jains)
216	Members of no religion[6]

Are only about one-third of human beings to be saved? Were all the rest created for nothing? Is it somehow their fault that they are not Christians? The mixing of people of every religious persuasion today has given us personal experience of the deep goodness of many who lie entirely outside the sphere of Christian influence. They love and follow other holy men and women of history, some of whom they believe to be true incarnations of God also. Our knowledge of their sacred writings and religious practices has shown us how sound and spiritually fruitful these writings and practices are. In fact, they are remarkably similar to our own! It is simply impossible to write non-Christians off as people living in darkness, unthinkable to consign them all to eternal damnation. Isn't there some way of understanding Jesus' relationship to God, and the relationship of other eminently holy men and women of history to God, which would make better sense of this total picture?

• *Our experience of God's immensity, incomprehensibility, and hiddenness make it very hard for us to believe that Jesus or any other human person could possibly be God.* In today's universe, it is far harder to domesticate God the way people were able to in the much smaller world of the first Christian centuries. Whatever the great Mystery is that lies hidden within the vast evolving cosmos, it is hard for us to believe that it can be fully expressed in a mere human person, however eminent that individual. It seems a little like trying to get the ocean into a pail. The incarnation must mean something other than that God came to earth and lived as a human person awhile, then returned to heaven. That sounds like mythology. This presentation of the matter also implies that God is not usually here, though Christian theology has always held that God is everywhere, present and active and incessantly manifesting the divine self in everything.

• *New Testament scholars themselves are having difficulty with the usual way of presenting the matter.* A critical reading of the New Testament shows how rarely it speaks of Jesus as God. Jesus never calls himself God. And those who write of him call him typically by much humbler names: prophet, rabbi (teacher), wisdom of God, servant of God, word of God, son of God, anointed one (that is what both "Messiah" and "Christ" mean, a person anointed by God to do a special work), holy one, master or lord (simply titles of respect). In only two clear instances does the New Testament call Jesus "God" (the Greek word *theos*), and both are in the gospel written last (Jn 1:1 in conjunction with Jn 1:14, and Jn 20:28).[7] The first three gospels never call Jesus God.

Theologians are well aware of these questions and difficulties. Many of them are teachers, in constant dialogue. All are dedicated readers, another form of dialogue. And as individuals themselves living in the contemporary situation, they come up against these issues in their own experience and reflection. One of theology's tasks is to keep reformulating the tradition, to find new ways of presenting it so that it speaks clearly, compellingly, and in a manner compatible with the advancing knowledge of each succeeding age. The tradition must also be adapted to diverse cultures. All of these considerations have led to a contemporary reformulation of the relationship between Jesus and God.

Rudolph Bultmann is to modern New Testament study what Sigmund Freud is to modern psychology. His historical/critical research into the New Testament has given us quite a different perspective on our scriptures. We now know the gospels to be many-layered accounts of the career of Jesus—history, yes, but with rich overlays of subsequent theological interpretation strongly coloring the story that comes down to us.[8] When Bultmann, Lutheran pastor as well as scholar, was asked whether Jesus is God, his answer was: Jesus is God for us. For him, this slight modification of the traditional formulation by the addition of two words perfectly expresses what the New Testament says. It could also be put this way: Jesus is God for all practical purposes, or as far as we are concerned. In other words, there is a *functional* identity between Jesus and God. Jesus' words are God's words, his actions God's actions, and in following him it is God whom we follow. But this is quite different from saying, Jesus is God, period, as if to assert an *ontological* identity. That the New Testament does not do.

Much theological thinking today follows a similar path. Another way the relationship is sometimes reformulated is by changing the traditional expression "Jesus, God *and* man," to "Jesus, God *in* man," or, in more inclusive language, "Jesus, God in a human being." So instead of thinking of Jesus as a different sort of person than we are, a person with two natures, divine and human, we might think of him as a human person like ourselves, but one in whom God dwells and acts in an amazing way. Every human being enjoys a divine indwelling. What makes Jesus extraordinary is the degree to which his being and whole life are permeated by God. This is partly God's doing. It also depends crucially on Jesus' free choice and cooperation. Since his deepest desire is to give his whole life to God, and he keeps choosing that even as its costs unfold, people experience from first to last a patent and powerful presence and activity of God in him. He is a window into God. He gives God a human face. Even now, risen from death and living a new life, his status as revealer, mediator, sacrament of God continues. Functionally, he is still God for us.[9]

The question then arises: Is he the only one who can function in this way? Our contemporary experience seems to challenge the Christian tradition here. We know that there have been other eminent sacraments or embodiments of God—great teachers, holy women and men, enlightened and inspired historical figures. They too have taught ways of wisdom and holiness, and lived what they taught in compelling ways.

Countless people have been and are today immensely helped by their legacies. These individuals too seem to be mediators of the Mystery for those who know and follow them.[10]

Well, is Jesus at least the greatest of them all? Who can say? Who has sufficient knowledge and the objectivity to judge? If we cannot judge on the basis of our knowledge today, can Jesus' companions of the first century, whose knowledge was far more constricted than ours, have made that judgment competently? It seems not. They write within a limited cultural horizon. And their writing betrays their immense *enthusiasm* for him rather than some sort of scientific objectivity—if so cool a stance were even possible in speaking of a person who has completely changed your life.

What Is the "Salvation" Jesus Offers Us?

Spiritual pilgrims, trying to relate to Jesus, also raise questions about the idea that he died for our sins. Difficulties range from the feeling that this just does not speak to us today, to some real problems with the image of God implied in the usual presentation of the matter.

When I ask classes of adult Christians, as I have many times, the open question of how Jesus is of help to them, I get a good fifteen or twenty answers before anyone says, "He died for my sins," and often I do not get that answer at all. My students are all mature Christians, people serious enough about their faith to have devoted their lives to Christian ministry. All of them have a relationship with Jesus, and are speaking from their actual experience of Christian existence. What they say about the difference Jesus makes in their lives, and this is another way of saying what "salvation" means, are things like this:

He shows me who God is.

He teaches me what God wants from me.

He accepts me as I am, and gently moves me to grow.

He shows me what life is all about: union with God and loving relationships with everyone.

He inspires me with courage and hope in the face of suffering.

He is the resource I call on when I am in need.

He is my friend.

He gives my life direction.

He brings God near, gives God a human face.

He promises me a life beyond this one, which is my real fulfillment.

He started and still inspires the community that is such a great help to me.

He has a program that would solve the world's problems—the poverty, the wars, all the alienations.

This is quite a catalogue of benefits, all directly from people's actual experience.

There have been times in Christian history when people had a heavy sense of their sinfulness and wondered if they could be forgiven or ever accepted by God. This is not the general feeling today, and so it seems the idea that "Jesus died for your sins" is a poor starting place for explicating his relevance to our lives. We do have a sense of what our real problems are. Why not start there? Jesus does speak to those, as the respondents above attest.

When the idea that he died for our sins comes under actual discussion, people express problems with the image of God being presented. What kind of God is this who demands the tortured death of a human being to assuage His *(sic)* anger? Many human beings, when they are wronged, do better than this. They absorb offenses and simply forgive, no revenge, no payback required. Surely God is a greater lover than we. Doesn't the tradition hold that God *is* love?

And isn't it this gracious God whom Jesus both describes and incarnates? To take a single example from his teaching, consider his portrayal of God in the parable of the prodigal son. The father in the parable demands no reparation when his wayward son returns to him. He has been waiting for him with love and longing all during his absence. He cuts short his son's embarrassed confession and throws him a party.

Where does the idea that Jesus died for our sins originate? Mainly from St. Paul. Not from Jesus himself. He never made a point about making satisfaction for sin by his death.[11] To Paul, though, this seemed a ready way to interpret, retrospectively, the significance of Jesus' death and resurrection. Why? The Jewish people had a long tradition of offering sacrifice to God to make satisfaction for their sins. And Paul had a profound sense of the sinfulness of all humanity. He makes it the starting point in his most systematic theological treatise, his Letter to the Romans. Now he reflects on yet another sacrifice, Jesus' death, certainly the greatest sacrifice of all. Surely God would be pleased. So in several places Paul presents Jesus' death in this light. What we have to recognize is that he is speaking *metaphorically*: There are some parallels, he is saying, between the Jewish tradition of sacrifices for sin and the crucifixion of Jesus.

The "satisfaction theory," as it came to be called, got its biggest boost in the Middle Ages when St. Anselm of Canterbury took this metaphor very literally and elaborated it into a theology. He went all the way back to the sin of Adam, which he said had provoked the wrath of God against all humanity and closed the gates of heaven. Someone had to make reparation, and because the offense was infinite, only an infinite being could do it. So the second Person of the Blessed Trinity volunteered to come down from heaven and become man in order to die on the cross for the sin of Adam and all subsequent sins. God was satisfied by this sacrifice, and the gates of heaven were reopened. Anselm's theory was taken over by St. Thomas Aquinas, whose presentation of the faith became normative for the Roman Catholic church until about the middle of the twentieth century. Martin Luther also embraced the central concepts and passed them on.

Today many theologians are moving away from this theory. This is partly because it seems to have been no part of Jesus' own sense of his mission and partly because it labors under the difficulties we have noted. In the New Testament, even in Paul's writings taken as a whole, it is a God of immense graciousness toward humankind, not an angry or alienated God, who stands behind Jesus' warm outreach to everyone. It all happens by God's initiative. Paul summarizes it this way:

> God was in Christ, reconciling the world to the divine self, *not counting people's offenses against them,* and God has entrusted to us this message of reconciliation. (2 Cor 5:19, italics mine)

So, where the question of salvation is concerned, whether we go back to the gospels and watch what Jesus does for the people around him or consult our own experience of what he does for us, we will find a much richer tapestry of life saving help than the satisfaction theory details. *All* of it, not just his death, is immensely helpful to us. If we restore to the sacrifice-for-sin idea its status as metaphor, and view it as just one of many possible perspectives on how the life, death, and resurrection of

Jesus are salvific for us, we will be getting a much truer picture of all we have from this incomparable benefactor of humankind.[12]

Questions and Exercises

1. This chapter attempts to rethink Jesus for the contemporary context, as an earlier chapter did for God. What in it is new to you? What do you agree with, and why? What do you disagree with, and why?

2. What role, if any, does Jesus play in your spiritual life?

3. Why do Christians set so much store by the death and resurrection of Jesus? What meaning do these events have for you personally?

4. Read any two consecutive chapters of any of the four gospels (except the first two chapters of Matthew or Luke, which tell of Jesus' infancy only) and journal about everything that strikes you.

5. With some friends, do a comparative study of Jesus in film. Watch, for example, *Jesus of Nazareth*, *Jesus Christ Superstar*, *The Last Temptation of Christ*, *Jesus of Montreal*. After viewing each, discuss the main features of each portrayal. Which appeals to you the most, which the least, and why?

Chapter Six

Is a Relationship with the Mystery Possible for Me?

Earth's crammed with heaven,
And every common bush afire with God:
But only he who sees takes off his shoes.
—*Elizabeth Barrett Browning*

We saw in the last chapter how intimate Jesus was with God. Is anything like the relationship he enjoyed possible for us?

He insisted that it is. A good bit of his energy went into telling people that the God he preached was available for, and indeed sought, a relationship with everyone. We can either relate *directly* to the God Jesus made known, the One he called "Abba." Or we can relate to God *through* Jesus. That is the point of the incarnation: God is present and active in Jesus, so that in seeing him we see God, and in loving and following him we love and follow God. This latter way has strong appeal for many, as it gives God a human face. A woman, seventy-seven, a widow, writes of her relationship with God in Jesus:

I have a picture of the "Joyous Christ" in my living room, and when I look at it I feel so close to Him and I can discuss any problems with Him. The twinkle in His eyes helps me remember that life doesn't have to be burdensome and the beautiful smile is one of love. Several times I have felt Him talking to me through that picture....He is my best friend!

Besides encounters with the God of Jesus in the words of scripture, in the sacraments, and in personal prayer, I would like to develop at some length four ways in which we encounter and relate to God as we move through our days engaged with the world. It is to these less "religious" ways of meeting God that most of us need to be alerted, because we can so easily miss them. Yet if God is the soul of the cosmos, it should come as no surprise that God can turn up anywhere, even in the most ordinary places and situations. "God is not far from any of us," Paul says, "for in God we live, and move, and have our being (Acts 17). God's relationship with the world can be expressed either way: All things are in God, or God is in all things.

The kinds of encounters I mean are as follows, three of them ordinary, one extraordinary:

1. We experience God wherever we experience goodness, beauty, or depth;
2. We experience God wherever we come up against our limits: our smallness, powerlessness, bafflement, discontent, mortality;
3. We experience God wherever we feel an inner nudge toward doing the good;
4. We also experience God in very special moments, which take us by surprise.

I speak of the *experience* of God. I am not attempting to mount arguments for the *existence* of God, which can be found in other places.[1]

We Experience God wherever We Experience Goodness, Beauty, or Depth.

If God is the source of all reality and is good, we might expect to glimpse more of God where we see goodness and beauty "gathered to a greatness," in the felicitous phrase of Gerard Manley Hopkins. And people always have. They tell us how they see God in the glory of the sunset, the majesty of the mountain, the expanse of the ocean. They get the feel of God when they are put in mind of the vastness of the cosmos—the staggering number of stars and the dimensions of the space in which they move. They feel the same awe when they learn of the aeons of time over which reality as we know it has evolved, from the simplest elements to the great complexities we find on planet earth. We can also come down to the little things, and the same Mystery communicates itself there as well. The rose, the newborn baby, the goodness of food, the beauty of one's beloved or of one's child. Where there is goodness, beauty, depth, there God is described—the Creative Genius, the Life in the Root. Two women describe their experiences:

> I find God in the beauties of nature, in the unfolding of a flower, in an exquisite sunrise, in the peace of a full moon. God is present in my dog's begging brown eyes and my kitty's jumping up to sleep cradled next to me at night.

> I experience God in nature—magnificent vistas, oceans, mountains, Grand Canyon, etc. But also the barrenness of

the desert, a winter landscape, flat farmlands of North Dakota. These experiences often put my own personal life in perspective.

The ancient Greeks, those creators of so much that is best in Western civilization, saw a god or goddess in every important area of life. There was one in the sea, one in the fields, one at the hearth. There was one in the sun, another in the moon. There was one for love and another one for war. Christians have sometimes mocked at this crude polytheism. But what it exhibits is an awesome sense of the Sacred. To the Greeks, everything was holy. Everything was charged with Mystery and deserved reverence. Wherever there was goodness, power, beauty, depth, the Greeks saw goddess or god.

Edith Hamilton, incisive student of all things Greek, contrasts the way the Greek artist portrayed the divine and the way the Hindu artist did it, their spiritual visions being so different. The Hindu artist, having no real interest in this world which he/she regarded as mere illusion, depicted the other world in symbols of an esoteric sort, creating statues with many arms, many hands, many heads. Greek spirituality went a different direction.

> The Greek artist thought neither of Heaven nor of Hell; the Word was very nigh unto him [sic]; he felt the real world completely sufficient for the demands of the spirit. He had no wish to mark the images of his gods with strange, unearthly attributes to lift them away from earth. He had no wish to alter them at all from what he saw as most beautiful, the shapes of the human beings around him....The Olympic Hermes is a perfectly beautiful human being, no more, no less. Every detail of his body was shaped from a consummate knowledge of

actual bodies. Nothing is added to mark his deity, no aureole around his head, no mystic staff, no hint that here is he who guides the soul to death. The significance of the statue to the Greek artist, the mark of the divinity, was its beauty, only that.[2]

Why speak of God here, someone might ask, when what we are remarking is simply the world's beauty? Why did the Greeks? Why are we not content simply to enjoy the rose or the baby or the vast universe, let them be themselves, and leave the gods out of it? One can indeed stop there, which is why we have agnostics and atheists in the world—as well as inside our own heads. I often see no more than the surfaces of things myself. But when I do, it is when I am less, not more, aware. In times I much prefer, when "the ear of my ear awakes and the eye of my eye is opened," as e.e. Cummings puts it, I see into and through to the depths, and feel a contact with the More. That is when I am most alive. A woman in her forties puts it this way.

> I much prefer the words "Great Mystery" or "Great Spirit" because "God" tends to conjure up Old Testament images which hook right into my experience of my physical father....When I slow down, tune in, listen, am present, then I am more likely to feel the caress of spirit in the wind, feel the heart of spirit in music, share the laughter and tears of spirit with others, channel the energy of spirit in massage.

This is what constitutes the religious experience, this getting beneath the surfaces of things, whether we think of it as our breaking through, or the Other Side breaking through to us and finally getting our attention. The key from our side is presence, receptivity, a slowing down, as this woman puts it. Then we realize that this entire reality in which we live is a symbolic reality, the expression of Something greater than itself, Something at once hidden and revealed. God is "the Beyond in our midst," it has been said. We have religious experience when we awaken to this Beyond. The only trouble with this term for God is its suggestion that God is distant, usually inaccessible. That is why I prefer to call God the Depth in things, and point deep down rather than beyond. God is *within*, and when we penetrate the surface, we find God.

If God is in the depths of all reality, then God is in our own depths as well. This is why we have so much religious experience in our relationships with one another. And it is a good thing we do, because so many of us live in cities and do not see a great deal of nature. A man in his fifties, a counselor, writes:

> I have a few good friends with whom I can discuss my real inner experience. Our sharing is community. And in that community is God. I have had spiritual experiences on my own when I had a moment of deep sharing with a friend, a meal that had the sense of the sacred, a spark of laughter with someone whose soul touched mine, a poem that brought me deeper into the mystery of life. And sometimes in my work with delinquent kids and staff, I have an experience of the power of divine love coming through me to them. I am the lightning rod, not the lightning, and what comes through me to them, often after periods of struggle and confusion, takes a healing shape that I did not imagine.

A woman who does administration speaks of yet other people-experiences in which God is present:

> I experience God with children—the sense of wonder, the awareness of potentiality, the openness, the sense of immediacy, in the present....Being with the elderly, especially

those in the final stages, is a godly experience for me. It puts me in touch with the ultimate meaning of life. The elderly have a quality of "beingness" and in those elderly years the quality of the "beingness" is often indicative of the life that preceded the present state.

The interactions these people recount are ordinary, but they are describing how sometimes the depths open up and the ground on which they stand together is holy. A younger married woman puts it this way:

God in my everyday life is the unexplainable spirit which vibrates through all the life around me. It is the tight hugs from my son, the new words he said today, the new feats he can perform. It is the student who surprisingly thanked me for helping her. It's the man who stopped to help the old lady who fell. It is the love I have for my son, husband, and family. It is the new life growing inside me.

These are all varying descriptions of human loving, which confirm from personal experience St. John's dynamite description of God in three words, and the immense consequence he goes on to name:

God is love, and the person who abides in love abides in God, and God in him or her. (1 Jn 4:16, italics mine)

It is love that keeps the world going, and where love is being given and received, God is present and active. A woman seventy, mother of six, in answer to my question about religious experience, simply says: "Childbirth, each and every time."

But there might be a difficulty with this emphasis on seeing through things to their depths, a possible misdirection. Trying to see *through* things could easily lead to not seeing them. And if we do not really see, hear, feel, smell, touch the reality most available to us, we will never glimpse the Depth or Beyond of it. Buddhist spirituality has been especially vigilant in promoting *mindfulness*, which means really being in the here and now, fully aware of what we are doing and experiencing, totally present. That means really *eating* our rice, every mouthful of it, every chew. That means really *taking* the shower, not thinking while showering of all we have to do that day so that the shower is over and we were never really there. It means *getting your head into the game*, as they say in baseball, playing with full concentration and intensity as if there were nothing else on earth but this game, indeed, this inning, this at-bat, this pitch. It means really being present to this conversation, as if all else stood still. Only when we are thus attuned to the here and now are we in a position to catch the aura around it, or its depth dimension—the Beyond in our midst. A story from the wisdom tradition illustrates the point.

> At a sacred site near the sea, legend had it that if one listened very closely, one could hear the most exquisitely beautiful chimes sounding from somewhere deep inside the sea. A devout man traveled thousands of miles to have this experience. Taking up the lotus position on the shore, he closed his eyes and listened intently. But all he could hear was the roar of the waves. He tried to push this aside, and penetrate to the holy sound. But to no avail. Determined, he kept at his task for several weeks. Finally, totally defeated, he decided to give it up. Perhaps he was simply not destined for this blessed experience. It was his final day, and he went to say good-by to the sea and sky and wind and coconut trees. He lay on the sands, listening to the roar of the waves. This time he did not resist it, but gave himself over

to it, and it produced a profound silence in his heart. Then, in the depth of the silence, he heard it—the tinkle of a tiny bell, followed by another and another and another, until a thousand temple bells were pealing out in glorious unison, transporting his heart with wonder and joy.

Wonder is the basis of worship. And wonder arises naturally when we are awake. Almost anything might put us in awe if we are really present to it. One of the hazards of modern life is that we do not really see, hear, or feel very much. We are too busy, too much in a hurry to get things done. Our technological, consumerist orientation has conditioned us besides to size things up for their practical utility to us. When we are sizing up for usefulness, we are not contemplating. Contemplation merely gazes, with no self-interest. The child is naturally contemplative, filled with wonder at the simplest things. The child is a parable for us. If we would live with God, we need to undergo a rebirth of wonder and recover our childlike contemplation. Contemplation and mindfulness are different names for the same basic stance toward reality.

A priest friend of mine runs a rustic retreat center. People come there for a weekend, sometimes a full week, not for any structured program, but just for the chance to be quiet in a natural setting where they and others seek to be with God. The only community gatherings are for daily eucharist late in the afternoon, followed by dinner. I asked him one time if he does a lot of counseling there. "Not much, really," he said; "I'm available, but most people don't need much. If they just come away from their ordinary routine, slow down, get quiet, spend some time in nature, they find God. And then their lives fall into place. They almost all come with problems, but after a day or two they come to peace with their problems or see a solution. It all happens without me." What a nice formula for spiritual regrounding: Return to nature, slow down, be quiet; you will become aware of God with you, and the pieces will fall into place.

We Experience God wherever We Come Up against our Limits: Our Smallness, Powerlessness, Bafflement, Discontent, Mortality.

The experiences described so far have all been positive—goodness, beauty, depth. We have another whole set of experiences, no less common, which constitute another avenue of religious experience. There is plenty of pain in life—the limitations of all there is, the restless discontent within, the abiding loneliness, the gnawing question one always is to oneself: Who and what am I anyway, and what is life all about? Then there are the more particular sufferings we bear—sickness, injury, never-ending work, the failure of relationships, depression, worry about money, anxiety about people we love, aging, the approach of death. Hamlet strips the question to the bone: To be or not to be?

> For who would bear the whips and scorns of time,
> The oppressor's wrong, the proud man's contumely,
> The pangs of despised love, the law's delay,
> The insolence of office, and the spurns
> That patient merit of the unworthy takes,
> When he himself might his quietus make
> With a bare bodkin? Who would fardels bear,
> To grunt and sweat under a weary life,
> But that the dread of something after death—
> The undiscovered country from whose bourn

No traveller returns—puzzles the will,
And makes us rather bear those ills we have
Than fly to others that we know not of?
                    (*Hamlet*, Act III, scene 1)

All these experiences, common, recurrent, really press the question of meaning. Where is God in all this pain? Again, by abundant testimony, paradoxical though it be, God is somewhere within it, or hovering right around it. A woman writes:

> I was in a long period of extreme emotional, psychological, spiritual darkness. I felt suicidal. Then I met someone who was able to be with me in that dark place and whose care and presence offered hope. I remember writing, "Between the dark night and the longed for day I live, suspended in hope. Elude me not, O promise of morning." One night shortly thereafter there was a violent rain and wind which lasted all night long and matched *exactly* the state of my psyche. I slept little that night, and when I got up in the morning I looked outside and was awestruck by the absolute clarity of the air, so much so that I couldn't move. Then from somewhere within/without I heard the words, "You will see clearly again, Mary. You will pass through this darkness and into a new light."

Notice how she instinctively prays through her trial. What else can one do? In this state of prayer she begins to sense God communicating with her through nature. God is mediated to her also through the indispensable help she receives from someone who stands with her in her struggle though unable to take it away. Finally there are the words she hears God saying to her. There is no relief yet, but the very promise of relief consoles her, telling her God is with her and her experience of darkness is somehow meaningful.

We may have an abiding sense of God. But it is usually when our pain is most intense that we find ourselves most concerned with God, most prayerful, and therefore also most in relationship. "There are no atheists in the foxholes," a popular saying has it. "Oh God!" is our instinctive cry when the mortars start falling around us. Does God suddenly appear now from out of the blue? Does the individual now become religious for the first time? No. God was always around, and the person always knew it; but now they really need God. A woman, seventy-five, writes of a time she will never forget:

> During World War II my husband was picked up by the Japanese and put in prison as a suspected guerrilla. Knowing the Japanese by then, I immediately started a forty-day novena to St. Jude, the saint for desperate and impossible cases, and went to mass and communion daily, praying for his release. Two weeks later we found the prison where he was, but could not see him. The man in charge kept saying they did not know when or if he would be released. Believe it or not, on the fortieth day of my novena, this same man pedalled in front of my house, where I happened to be sitting on the porch, and I called him to stop. He did and told me to come five days later with clothes for my husband. I did and the Japanese actually released him looking like a Dachau inmate but *alive!*

This woman will always remember the nearly miraculous restoration of her husband to her as an incredible gift, and the answer to her unremitting prayer. What interests me even more in her story is the simple fact of her total dedication to prayer in her time of desperation, and the significance of that. Think of how many people in her situation have prayed for someone's release or restoration and never gotten it. Yet their prayer seems very meaningful to me. Often prayer is the only expression available to us of the love we have for someone. It is our bond of unity with them. Praying for someone, sending them love-energy, and being bonded with them in spite of separation, seem to me, all three, one and the same thing.

Times of crisis aside, there is an abiding experience of our smallness, powerlessness, mortality, and discontent running right down the middle of lives many of us would probably describe as quite rich. This nagging distress is first of all a pointer toward God as our true fulfillment, a destiny beyond the sum total of all this world has to offer. It orients us toward life after death as our longed-for consummation. But it might well also mean that we need more of God right now. "All religion begins with the cry 'Help!'" philosopher William James declares in his *Varieties of Religious Experience*. He is right. Religion's defining product is salvation. James goes on:

> The warring gods and formulas of the various religions do indeed cancel each other, but there is a certain uniform deliverance in which religions all appear to meet. It consists of two parts: (1) an uneasiness, and (2) its solution. 1. The uneasiness, reduced to its simplest terms, is a sense that there is *something* wrong *about us* as we naturally stand. 2. The solution is a sense that we *are saved from the wrongness* by making proper connnection with the higher powers.[3]

Veterans of the spiritual life attest that it is in the good times, not the bad, that we most need to work on our relationship with God. In the bad times, we are almost automatically God-conscious. In the good times, we tend to forget about God, and just take everything for granted.

When a friend read over my first draft for this book, his comment was that most of the religious experiences people recounted were of the God of the sunset and the mountain. "I meet God in the dark and dreadful hour," he said, "when I am brought up against the pain of my existence. Write about the Twelve Steps the alcoholic takes as he tries to recover, especially that first step, in which he admits that he is completely powerless. We're all alcoholics, really. Spirituality is for me not a matter of life enhancement. It is a matter of life or death."

Karl Rahner suggests that when we are feeling really lonely, if we are brave enough to resist the urge to call someone up, or go shopping, or take a drug, or turn on music or TV, or go to bed; if we are courageous enough to remain alone and, instead of fleeing the pain, to go down into it; we will gradually notice another Presence there, silent but benevolent and peaceful. I have tried it. He is right. And when I sit there awhile with that quiet Presence, I feel somehow consoled and able to go on, though no words are spoken and outwardly not a thing has changed.

The hard times throw us on God. And if we look, God is there for us. A woman, sixty-five, writes of what happened after her divorce:

> My forty-two year marriage broke up and it has been my twice daily meditation that has sustained me. I've truly learned to love silence and solitude and the experience of the hidden God. I can fully appreciate Meister Eckhart's saying: "There is nothing in all of creation that is so much like God as silence." I'm also learning that God speaks to me in my dreams, and I'm very touched by what I consider a tangible sign of God's concern with my well-being.

Is a Relationship with the Mystery Possible for Me?

A hospice nurse writes of what she sees in some of the very sick people with whom she works.

> I see glimpses of the suffering Jesus in my terminally ill patients. I am touched by the courage and faith I witness in them. God is very present to many I see. The faith is most evident in the Hispanic and African American patients, who are usually most expressive of their faith.

Another woman, who lost her daughter tragically, writes:

> Now that I have stopped hating God, I am very aware that I experience God every moment of every day. Both inside and out. It's not always conscious, but always bubbling beneath the surface. In my students, my friends, my family, myself. Usually in people, and when I'm writing.

Would she have this kind of awareness or be this interested in God had she not suffered this tragedy? Would the terminally ill be so God-focused if they had not been rudely brought up against their mortality? Possibly. But our own experience confirms that there is nothing quite as effective as pain at getting us to reground ourselves in the Saving Presence, which is always already there.

A homemaker, trying to cope with the pain of her life while on a retreat, recounts this experience.

> I was trying to meet Jesus in various scriptures, but the crowds were always there. I got discouraged and went and sat on a rock on the beach. Jesus came and saw me and asked what I wanted. I said, "Will you heal me?" He looked at me and said, "No." I cried and he said, "What you are asking is the work of a lifetime. You need to go

through it to be healed." And I knew the truth of his words.

She is disappointed not to find what she is seeking on her retreat, nor even to get what she asks Jesus for directly. What she gets instead is a profound insight, a kind of total orientation toward life: It may be that life itself, all of it—agony, ecstasy, and sheer plod—borne and lived through, is God's way of healing us.

We Experience God wherever We Feel an Inner Nudge toward Doing the Good.

This is actually a fairly constant relationship to the Transcendent, and it probably has greater significance for our spiritual life than the avenues so far mentioned. Yet it is rarely noted in treatments of religious experience. We experience God within ourselves prompting us to do the good.

Our response to this inner prompting is a crucial element in our spiritual life. It is always the direction of growth. Our response to it determines the kind of person we make of ourselves, which is exactly what we are most responsible for in life. That the quality of a person's moral/ethical life is the most reliable indication of a genuine spiritual life is shown by the fact that it is the first thing we look for in someone professing to be spiritual. Absent this, they lose credibility with us, whatever other religious experiences they may report and however elevated their discourse.

As I survey the human pageant, I observe that people generally finish better than they began. There is more quality of personhood in those who have lived awhile than in those not yet very far down the trail of the years. Reality somehow succeeds, by and large, in creating decent human beings. This is remarkable, especially when you consider how much evil there is in the world, and how many disasters of various shapes and sizes befall just about everybody. Or even how insufficiently loved most people are. I link this successful fashioning of decent human beings directly to God's ongoing creative endeavor. I deem it the area where God works with us most closely. The core of the face-to-face relationship with God is right here, in the privacy of our own inner consciousness, where we are constantly prompted to do the good. And most of the time we are scarcely aware that God is there or has anything to do with it. God seems happy enough hidden.

But why does a mother devote herself day in and day out to the care of her infants and children at such great personal cost? Why do one or both parents go out to the same dull job day after day to support the lives for which they are responsible? Why be responsible in the first place? It is easier not to. Yet parents typically spend more on their children than they do on themselves.

Or consider what many people today do for their aging parents. Inconvenient, demanding, often unappreciated, it is a labor of love. First they spent themselves on their children; now they spend themselves on their parents. Why bother? Yet most do it, and just consider it part of their responsibility. A man, fifty, writes:

> My big question is how to be loving to my aged mother who is, to me, quite unlovable.

A woman hospital administrator puts it this way:

> I don't think of God as an experience. I think it is how I treat people, and the positiveness and support I receive from others. I recently learned (I must have known this)

that I really do have a *choice* on how I behave and think,
and I think this is somehow related to God.

Take another example. Why do we honor the truth when so
often it would be easier not to? It is costly to tell the truth in a
lot of situations, yet something inside us tells us how important
it is that we do it. Similarly, it is often not easy to *hear* the truth
and honor it. In marriage, for instance, our mate often tells us a
truth about ourselves that we wince to hear. Far easier to throw
up our defenses, even mount a counterattack. But the truth is
bigger than this battle, larger even than this whole relationship.
It has a sort of transcendent claim on us, and we know it. The
truth and our convenience are often in conflict. What is this
inner prompting to reach past personal interest and be faithful
to the truth?

The businessman knows he should be basically honest. He is
not always, but when he is not he does not feel good about it; he
knows it is wrong. Husbands and wives, even the unmarried in
committed partnerships, know it is wrong to fool around sexually, though it is easy enough to do so. Always there is this
prompting within to do the right thing, the good thing, difficult
though it be. A homemaker writes:

> When I see my children struggle in their lives and grow, to
> me that is an experience of God. Working through the
> daily realities of growth, differences, struggles within our
> family is a constant experience of God. My relationship
> with my husband is an ongoing experience of God, both in
> our struggles and in our joys.

A woman, fifty-seven, former nun, now lay teacher and counselor, recounts the following experience of being interiorly

moved to do something that would require her whole life commitment:

> I was preparing a talk for a group of elementary school principals on the topic of social justice. It was evening and I was working away in a dormitory that was converted into an office. I was alone and really into the topic. The Bishops' Pastoral on Justice in the World really moved me, along with much that Peter Henriot had written. In the midst of preparing my talk I can remember that my eyes filled with tears and I knew, deep within me, that "action on behalf of justice, and participation in the transformation of the world, was truly constitutive of preaching the Gospel." I felt that very deeply, and believed that working for this was the deepest commitment I had ever made and it was this commitment that would shape my life.

That commitment still shapes her life.

Sometimes the inner prompting is not so much to do something as it is to *accept* something, something we do not want. Consider what human beings bear with. Sickness, injury, sometimes pain that never goes away. The difficulty of relationships—in school, in the workplace, at home, in the extended family. Depression. Anxiety. Loneliness. Failure. Rejection. The loss of loved ones. The injustice of social systems. The prejudices and oppression of others. Poverty. War. What keeps us going? Why don't we just pull down the shades and crawl into bed? Why aren't we all bitter, and the bitterer the longer we live? Why don't we simply end it?

For some reason, on the whole we opt to go on, bearing what we must, hoping for better things. We choose to bring children into the world. Even people whose lives are far more difficult than ours do. Whence the hope at the basis of this choice?

111

Consider too how remarkably some people reverse their heritage. Many who were harshly parented parent now with consummate kindness and generosity. People who were physically or sexually abused not only shield their children, but spend themselves trying to heal other victims, and are generous in love generally. What is it that keeps the light burning within, that has us hoping whatever our present suffering, that sustains us in loving when we could just as easily wreak on others the destruction that has been wrought on us?

I call it the divine within. I can think of no other explanation. Some Quiet Voice inside gives assurance that the struggle is worth it, that tomorrow is another day, that all shall be well. The same creative force which, since the Big Bang, has worked to bring into being more and more beauty in ever more complex configurations, is still at work in each person's life to make him or her more beautiful. And adversity seems to be a crucial part of the process. Stretching us, sometimes breaking us, comforting us, burning us, restoring us, knocking the corners off, smoothing the edges, ever sustaining us, refining and polishing, this Mysterious Force deep down keeps creating beauty. Gerard Manley Hopkins deftly describes this mystery of our transformation through pain:

> Sheer plod makes plow down sillion
> Shine, and blue-bleak embers, ah my dear,
> Fall, gall themselves, and gash gold-vermilion.
> ("The Windhover")

The Force co-creates, I should remark. Our cooperation is crucial. Not everybody becomes beautiful. Not every married couple works it out; some are sniping and snarling to the bitter end. Some individuals are more selfish than ever in their old age.

Others are bitter and negative, a trial to all who have to deal with them. Some people never become tolerant, or patient, or wise. No, it is not automatic. God's purpose is constant, but any of us can thwart it. That is why I call this moral/ethical arena the most important where the spiritual life is concerned, the one that really counts. God is a great gambler, passionate about the divine dream, but too respectful of creatures' autonomy to force anything. God's is a gentler mode—to invite, to draw, to nudge, always leaving us free to say our yes or no. It is as visionary and lover that philosopher Alfred North Whitehead portrays God:

> God is the poet of the world, with tender patience leading
> it by his (sic) vision of truth, beauty, and goodness.[4]

The test of an authentic spirituality is what kind of person it produces. The person desired is the sort we all instinctively and by common consent esteem—the one who is kind, patient, tolerant, generous, courageous, hopeful, positive, forgiving. It is the person who engages life wholeheartedly, who creates beauty and is him- or herself beautiful. No one is born so. Birth provides only the raw materials. Such qualities are perseveringly cultivated through a courageous grappling with the conditions of existence and a faithful responding to the still small voice that prompts us always to do what is good in the situation we are in. An older woman once remarked that, besides gratitude, there are just two kinds of prayer: for wisdom to know what to do, and for courage to do it. Another woman describes how God sometimes seems to direct her what to do.

> I have on occasion been spoken to by God concerning
> decisions I was to make. The voice is unmistakable, and the
> message is clear, although it is not audible. This kind of

experience happens more often after a problem has been "prayed through" and I begin to "rest" or relax about it. More often than not, the answer seems to appear when I am engaged in some menial chore.

Several people, in answer to my question, "How would you like to grow spiritually?" give essentially the same answer, bearing testimony to this same inner prompting:

> A woman, fifty-two, counselor: "I am seeking the form to offer service."

> A man, fifty-one, psychologist: "I want to make a difference, to help others."

> A man, thirty-three, professor: "I seek to discern God and God's plan—to do 'something great' with my life, which He has given to me."

> A woman, fifty-two, therapist: "What are we to do in our life for the good? That remains my spiritual question."

This is surely one of the principal ways we experience the presence of Spirit within us.

Special Moments

So far we have spoken of the three avenues of our ordinary, habitual experience of God. We come now to a category of special experiences, which quite a few people seem to have. They are brushes with the Mystery up close—powerful, unmistakable, unforgettable, sometimes of such potency as to change the whole course of a life. For example:

While I was praying, I was suddenly, but ever so softly, lifted from one realm to a much higher spiritual realm. From the bottom of my being it felt like a wellspring of such joy as is unknown in ordinary life. It began with a bubbling sensation and rolled out in a continuous bubbly laughter that I could not contain; nor did I want to. My arms refused to remain at my sides, but rather lifted of their own accord in spontaneous praise; I could not hold them still. When I tried to describe to those around me what I was experiencing my tongue was loosed, and I could only speak in a language that was unknown to me. Although I had always attended church and believed myself to be a Christian, my outlook was dramatically changed from that moment.

Sometimes a person is not praying at all, but just going about her business. A physician writes:

I had this *huge* overwhelming Spirit of Forgiveness/Compassion/Awareness of God my Father saying to me "I love you" one day while driving to work. I started crying and had to pull over for safety as I couldn't see or pay attention to traffic, while being washed in my own cleansing/releasing tears and joy.

Not only need one not be praying when such things happen; one need not even be an adult. A man writes of an extraordinary day in a very painful childhood.

When I was about eight or ten, I was walking across a field on a beautiful spring morning when I was suddenly "touched" by something. It felt like the lightest brush of an immensely powerful force—like a ten-volt shock coming from a billion-volt power plant. Still, it was

> enough to knock me down and send me sprawling. I felt simultaneously frightened and elated. The strangest part was that I was absolutely filled with an overwhelming sense of love, specifically that I was loved by God, a new experience for me since I did not feel loved by my family. At the same time, I was suddenly aware that God was the stuff of the universe, that everything was holy—grasshoppers, fish, birds, plants, people, everything. My stand as a conscientious objector dates from this experience, since in my heart of hearts I *know* that all violence is a violation of God's will.

The message in each of these experiences is the same: I love you. Simply that. All three persons testify to the amazing power of the love they felt.

The third report contains another element sometimes present in these encounters with the Divine—some sort of direction or vocation. In this case it was to have reverence for all living things, which bore fruit later in the man's life in the decision to be a conscientious objector.

The third account hints also at another feeling usually a component of these experiences: fear. In the 1920s, a German scholar, Rudolph Otto, made a careful study of the religious experience. In his classic, *The Idea of the Holy*, Otto describes what is encountered in such moments as "*mysterium tremendum et fascinosum*,"[5] which might be translated "a mystery terrible and wonderful." He goes on to describe our two primary reactions to it: We are at once attracted (*fascinosum*) and terrified (*tremendum*). We are surprised and delighted to be in the Presence, yet are also afraid. Biblical accounts of divine visitations usually express both these poles of the experience. One thinks of the angel's calming words to Mary the mother of Jesus in the story of the annunciation: "Do not be afraid" (Lk 1:31), which tell us that she was. So is Peter, right after the miraculous catch of fish. He has sensed what it is he is sitting with in that boat, and instinctively exclaims, "Depart from me, O Lord, for I am a sinful man!" (Lk 5:8). Does he really want Jesus to go away? No. But he is not exactly relaxed either. Jesus calms him, then missions him: "Do not be afraid. From now on, you will be a fisher of human beings" (Lk 5:10). A man of our own time reports an experience in which the fear was stronger than anything else.

> It was a time in my life when I doubted God or the whole necessity of living a spirit-filled life. This is the state I was in after leaving seminary. One morning about 5:30 AM, I experienced what I can only describe as a visit from the spirit-world. Although no words were spoken, I actually saw a "light" appear while this was taking place, and I received a definite message which has shaped my whole life since. But it scared the hell out of me. I was terrified, my whole body shaking, so much so that I did not tell a soul about this for years. I never want to experience anything like that again.

And yet this brief encounter changes everything, giving this man a clear sense of mission that shapes his whole life's dedication. Needless to say, it also sets aside his doubts about God's reality.

This same note of vocation or mission is the kernel of an account from a woman in childbirth.

> Thirty-one years ago I was giving birth to my third and last child. I was given a spinal anesthetic which produced an acute respiratory problem. I knew I was dying but it was, as many have said, very peaceful. I was letting go—I saw The Light—but my baby began to struggle in my womb

and it was as if she was knocking on the door trying to get out. I realized her struggle and thought about my other two daughters, who were two and four, and I made a conscious decision to live. I thought, "I must live to take care of all three of them." I prayed to live. Although I could not see or respond, I began to hear medical personnel making every effort to save me.

Sometimes the religious experience is neither an "I love you" nor a "Here is what I want you to do," but simply a miraculous opening of the eyes, like the healing of the blind man in the gospel (Jn 9).

> I was just looking out my bedroom window at a moonless night sky when suddenly I became aware that everything I was seeing was *alive*, including the air, the stars, and the dark trees. Later, I recognized the experience in two works of art, Van Gogh's *Starry Night* and Gerard Manley Hopkins's poem, "God's Grandeur."

A man, fifty-two, for some years a seminarian, now father and homemaker, catalogues a fascinating variety of special moments: Among the experiences of God that moved me most were:

1. The two weeks I spent with members of the United Farm Workers in the Fresno County jail in 1973;

2. A retreat with and for mentally retarded adults in 1974;

3. The adoption process of our fifth child, who was "blind";

4. Our decision to begin tithing to the church when we were dirt poor;

5. A four-day retreat in a maximum-security prison on a Kairos Team working with "the worst of the worst";

6. A day on Stinson Beach, laughing hilariously and at length with two good friends and my sister— an experience of the laughing God, one of the best;

7. God drenched me quite unexpectedly one week in '87 or '88 while I was living in Houston.

Striking in all these accounts is the careful individual tailoring of each person's experience, and the strong note of personality in the Mystery encountered. They are true I-Thous.

I close this inventory with a marvelous occurrence in the life of a woman, forty-seven, a massage therapist.

> I was swimming about a mile offshore in Hawaii with some friends. We were singing for dolphins to come play with us and suddenly caught sight of three humpback whales in the distance. They turned and headed straight for us. I felt exhilaration and fear at the same time, but nevertheless started swimming toward them. Next thing I knew these huge, beautiful, graceful creatures were swimming beneath me, then right next to me, close enough to reach out and touch. One of them swam head on toward me and I quickly turned, only to hear the creature say, "It's OK, you don't have to turn away." So I turned back and watched the trio, which appeared to be a family (mother, father, and baby). They swam around and among us, huge though they were, like the most graceful of dancers, an incredible manifestation of power and gentleness. Then the largest one swam right next to me, its eye looking straight into mine, and once again I heard it say directly to my heart, "Remember who you are."

Such experiences seem truly enviable. But there are many good people I know who have never had a single one. Theirs is a more plodding faith, which glimpses God only through a glass darkly. I myself have had only a very few of these special moments in my life. I've wanted many more, and thought maybe if I prayed more or managed somehow to become "holy," I might have them more regularly—but it was not to be. They are gratuitous gifts, completely at God's discretion. I have come to peace with that. It is a matter of letting God be God. Though these experiences are not uncommon, it seems that the larger number of people do not have them. In fact, some live their entire lives without any felt sense of the Presence, sometimes even with an abiding sense of a kind of absence. They wonder if they are doing something wrong. I do not think so. We cannot penetrate the mystery of God's dealings with each of us. All we can do is trust that whatever *is* is for the best. We do not really need special visitations to be good persons, which is the whole point of the spiritual life. They are the whipped cream on the sundae, the cherry in the manhattan.

To sum up, yes, live contact with the Mystery is possible! For some, there are special moments, close brushes with the Holy. In such encounters, God seems to say,

"I love you," or
"Here is what I want you to do," or
"Let me open your eyes to Reality."

Available to all of us is a low-level daily experience of God. From God's side, the Self-giving for relationship is a constant. But we can be oblivious to it. From our side, realizing the connection hinges on being awake, aware, attentive. Then comes the all-important factor, our free response. There seem to be three principal avenues of the encounter:

1. We experience God wherever we experience goodness, beauty, or depth. Here God seems to be saying, "Let me give you a glimpse of what I am like." The response? "You are amazing. Thank you."

2. We experience God wherever we come up against our limits: our smallness, powerlessness, bafflement, discontent, mortality. Here God seems to be saying, "It is I you are looking for. I am your salvation." The response? "Thank you. I do need you. I put my life in your hands."

3. We experience God wherever we feel an inner nudge toward doing the good. Here God seems to be saying, "Just do it." The response? "I will."

Questions and Exercises

1. Does a person have to go to church or say a prayer or read the Bible to be in relationship with God? If you answer no, then why go to church, pray, or read the Bible?

2. What is your own ordinary day-to-day experience of God? Does it come under any of the three ways described in this chapter?

3. Go back through your life and write up in your journal all the more vivid experiences of God that you can remember. What are your thoughts and feelings as you do this?

4. If yours has been a habitual experience of darkness and a felt absence of God in your life, is there any way this might be a gift or blessing in disguise?

5. Is there anything we can do to heighten our experience of God?

6. Why does this chapter take the position that God as the Inner Nudge toward doing the good is the most important of the avenues of religious experience? Do you agree?

Chapter Seven

Toward a Life-Giving Christian Spirituality: Ten Guiding Principles

> To tell the story of Jesus is to tell the final truth
> about the human story, and to tell the human
> story in its depth, as Jesus did, is to point to the
> mystery of God at the heart of human existence,
> to "name grace."
>
> —*Mary Catherine Hilkert*

Historically, many approaches to the spiritual life have grown from Christian roots. Most of them have been healthy. But it is undeniable that there have been unhealthy spiritualities as well.

The situation is the same today. If we survey the many ideas being presented about what it means to live the Christian life, we will find significantly varying images of God, readings of God's will, presentations of Jesus, and emphases on what constitutes the important features of a life lived in harmonious relationship with God.

As I work with people, I find myself frequently appealing to some ten principles that have crystallized for me over the years, convictions I regard as reliable and foundational for a life-giving, growth-producing Christian spirituality. They are solidly grounded in the Bible and the Jesus tradition, as I will show. They are also shaped by what I know of human psychology.[1] People seem to find them helpful for understanding their experience, aligning themselves with God, and making the important decisions they have to make in their lives. Let me set them forth.

1. God Wants Life for Us.

This is the first and most important principle of the series because it names God's fundamental stance toward us. In the Christian faith vision, God is for us. God stands on the side of life and of all that belongs to life—liberation, healing, expansion, well-being, growth, joy. We know this mostly from Jesus, and it is for obvious reasons called "good news," the meaning of "gospel." As the eminent Roman Catholic theologian Edward Schillebeeckx puts it, the human cause is God's cause.[2] God is for us.

In support of this contention, we could cite particular biblical texts. But the overarching witness is the entire biblical narrative. In it, from the first page to the last, God is working for humanity's good. Christians call the entire account "salvation history," because it is a string of stories of rescue from trouble. First, from primeval chaos, then from a state of slavery, then from being lost in a desert, then from hunger, then from opposing armies, God keeps saving people. God gives land. God gives direction (the Law) as to the purpose of human life and the kind of behavior that supports life for all. When, over time, powerful individuals oppress the people, God sends prophets to confront the oppressors and liberate the people. It is within this prophetic tradition that Jesus stands. He aligns himself with the poor and oppressed of society, confronts the wealthy and powerful, and spends himself in a ministry of healing and liberation in God's name. The moral of the entire biblical story is that God wants life for us. The divine purpose could hardly be clearer.

At the head of the book stands an image so positioned because it is cardinal. It is the image of a man and a woman in a lovely garden that has been given them for their enjoyment. A single stipulation is made, and it is for their safety. The whole of God's purpose is epitomized in this portrait (Gn 1–2). It is as if God said: "It's all for you. Have a good time."

Jesus' words are these: "I have come that they might have life, and have it to the full" (Jn 10:10). In one of his letters, John sums it up in three words: "God is love" (1 Jn 4:8).

Why lay stress on this point in a way so obvious? Because Christians themselves so often miss it. We are afraid to get mixed up with God because we fear God will take everything away from us! Christian spirituality itself has been the culprit in some of its representations, teaching that we should love the cross, that the harder thing is the better thing, that God sends us sufferings as a special mark of love. Jesus never said any of this. Where he saw suffering, he moved to alleviate it. His whole dedication was to the cause of life.

And so, wherever healing, reconciliation, liberation, wholeness, love, and joy are happening, God's purpose is being realized. A woman in her forties writes:

> It was on a retreat that I finally came to believe that God was really for me, really loved me as I was. It was a combination of many things. We were out in the country, and every day I walked in nature where everything spoke goodness and beauty to me. Another influence was that my retreat director guided me to many passages of scripture where God spoke love, even tenderness, and they touched

me in a way they never had before. But I think more than anything else it was my director herself who brought God's love home to me. She was so accepting, so encouraging, and so supportive of me just where I was that God somehow came through to me in a new way. Maybe God was not such a slavedriver after all, critical and demanding all the time. What a relief it was. Now that I know God differently, I'm a better lover myself.

2. The Purpose of Our Life Is to Learn How to Love.

Near the end of his public life, Jesus is asked what the greatest of God's commandments is. In answering, he sums up the whole Bible and all his own teaching: Love God with your whole heart, and love your neighbor as yourself (Mk 12:28–34). In John's gospel he offers a slight variation: "Love one another as I have loved you" (Jn 13:34). If this is his "Great Commandment," then it seems clear that to his way of thinking the very purpose of our lives is to learn how to love.

Our experience confirms him, telling us how central and supremely valuable love is. It is what makes life livable. How much we crave it, how much we want to give it, how greatly it helps in making life's difficulties bearable. We have also discovered how hard it is to love well. No matter where we are in the life span, we are doubtless still far from loving our enemies, far from taking the welfare of people not in our immediate circle much into account, far, alas, even from properly loving those who are closest to us. No wonder Jesus, surveying the pained human scene, reminds us so frequently that love is the answer.

It is not just others whom we find hard to love. We do not usually love ourselves much either, and need a push in that direction, for this too is part of the commandment. Many of us are far harder on ourselves than on anyone else. We criticize ourselves mercilessly, abuse our bodies, shy away from asking for what we need or want, submit meekly to mistreatment, disqualify ourselves in advance when a job or relationship we would like could be ours. For many Christians who love others quite generously, the hardest part of the commandment is learning to be good to themselves and also to receive the love that is given by others.

Practically every issue we struggle with in life comes down to love in some way. How should I deal with my husband or wife? How should we deal with this child? This parent? Should I stay in this relationship or leave it? Why am I so lonely? Do I have any real value? Any rights? How should I use what money and power I have? How should I vote? These are all questions about love, and love is at bottom a spiritual issue—the most important spiritual issue of all, the very purpose of life. So the question is, how will I make love the highest priority, balancing a genuine love for others with an appropriate love for myself?

If love is what we are made for, little wonder that we feel empty if we are not doing much of it. We can easily get centered on ourselves, and walk the world asking, "Who will love me?" We need to do an about-face and live from the question, "Whom can I love?" or "Who needs me?" Then we start finding meaning and satisfaction. Oddly, we get more love from others now too than we ever did when we were seeking it. "Give, and it will be given to you," Jesus suggests (Lk 6:38).

In every situation in life, a good question to ask is: If I view this situation with the eyes of love, what do I see and what do I do?

3. Where the Action in Our Life Is, God Is Present and Active.

If we are searching for God, the first place to look is wherever the action in our life is right now. That is the locus of the pivotal encounter. Are we struggling with sexual addiction? Then that is the area where we are most engaged with God. Are we working to overcome the damages of our childhood? Are we dueling with depression? Then there is probably nothing of greater significance in our relationship with God right now than these core struggles. God is always where the action is.

Why is this? Because God has a stake in what we make of ourselves, and the areas of our life that most absorb our attention are the areas of greatest consequence in that regard. That is where our energy is going, right? That is where we are making choices that have lasting consequences.

Spiritually, we want not only to be aware of God, but to make a good response. So the question is: What is the opportunity God is offering me here? What is God inviting or challenging me to? And what gift is God trying to give me?

I think of a man who fought the alcoholic battle all his life. I know him well because he was my father. Over the decades I watched the struggle shape him. His failures were the root of his humility, and the source of his abundant compassion. His struggle taught him self-awareness and an exacting self-discipline. He learned to be a truth-teller. His weakness threw him again and again on God, and carved the channels of his spiritual life. His need for human support led to friendships that profoundly influenced his becoming, and in which he gave much of his love and acquired wisdom. Was his alcoholism a curse or a blessing? Hard to say. Whatever it was in itself, he and God certainly made a blessing out of it. This core lifelong struggle of his was the place where he and God were most vitally engaged.

We somehow cling to the idea that spirituality is what happens when we are in church or reading our Bible. It is *really* happening always, especially in the areas of life where we are most challenged at any given time. When people describe their problems to me in therapy, I often ask: Where do you think God is in all this? Whatever brought them in is where the action is for them right now, and hence the arena of critical engagement.

4. God Does Not Send Us Pain and Suffering, but Works with Us in Them for Good.

There seems to be as much that is going wrong in this world of ours as is going right, and massive suffering is the plainest fact. This is an enigma, especially if we believe in a good and caring God. For all of us, life is always a struggle, as we must do many things we do not wish to do and bear many things we do not wish to bear. Why does life have to be so difficult?

The point of this principle is to state clearly where God stands with respect to our suffering. It is not God who willed or caused our sexual abuse as children. It is not God who "sends" us cancer or AIDS. It is not God who brought about our divorce, "took" our child, caused us to be lonely, or decided to make us poor. Otherwise God is part of the problem, not of the solution.

Where then *is* God in these events that cause us so much pain? First, God is at our side grieving with us, as anyone who loves us would. Second, God is working with us to bring forth all possible good from the evils we suffer. Third, God is calling all of us to change the conditions that produce these evils. The fact is, it is what we human beings do to ourselves and to each other that produces almost all the suffering we bear.

God, as creator, stands at the source of the reality in which we live, and to that extent is responsible for everything. But God's decision was to make a world genuinely distinct from self, and so to create it free. This means there is much that God cannot control, whether to prevent or to produce. Freedom exists in some measure even in the simplest entities in the universe. It is particularly broad at the human level. An immense amount of what goes on in the world depends on free, created agency, and it is from bad human choices that the bulk of our pain and suffering come, both in individual cases and in the larger socioeconomic systems that set the conditions framing our lives.[3]

The symbol of the cross has so often been viewed by Christian spirituality as a sign that God's *plan* is pain and suffering, that God *sends* us travail as trial or as punishment, that the holy response is to *embrace* it with gratitude or at least with resignation. But, as we saw in the last chapter, this line of thinking fails to distinguish Jesus' whole thrust from the fate that befell him. He poured his energies not into getting up on a cross, but into freeing people from what ailed them and teaching them how to live. He did this because he saw it as *God's* project and purpose. He was killed not out of God's design but out of human malice.

What then is the Christian response to suffering, in our own or others' lives? Our first response should be to try to remove it, as Jesus did. In this we join our energies and purpose with God's own. Only when we have done everything we can to overcome suffering should we accept the unsolved remainder, placing our trust in God, who works with us to draw out of suffering all possible good.

5. The Paradigm of Death and Resurrection Is Key to Understanding Our Existence.

The death and resurrection of Jesus is the core around which Christian faith revolves. As we saw in the last chapter, it is for Christians a paradigm, as the Exodus is for Jews: both are paradigms of hope in the midst of adversity. And so both are continually commemorated ritually to support the life of faith. In our daily experience, we are thoroughly familiar with the realities of suffering and death. What we need is a reason to hope. The death and resurrection of Jesus gives us that reason, revealing to us that with God death is never the last word. Life is.

Many times in life, we are either dying or need a push because we need to die. Obviously, I am speaking of more than the death of the body at the end of our life. I am speaking of what *feels* like death—losing whatever it is that seems like life itself to us. So we die when we lose a loved one, when we are oppressed and cannot be ourselves, when we see someone we love suffer and can find no way to help them, when we are beset with depression and cannot seem to get out of it, when we face the diminishments and losses of the aging process. In such times, we need to hear of resurrection from death, the good news that God is at work in all this dying to bring new life out of it. Of this mystery, the death and resurrection of Jesus is the paradigmatic instance.

There are other moments in life when we absolutely have to die to find new life, and we do not want to do it. This is when we need to hear about the death-pole of the paradigm, death as the sine qua non for new life. The death in question might be finally letting go of a relationship that has proved to be a dead end so that we can be open to a new relationship. It might be taking the awful risk of letting someone know who we really are, so that we can learn what real love is. It might be putting away our addictive substance and taking our first shaky steps without it. It might be surrendering manipulative efforts to get people to love us, choosing simply to be ourselves instead and take our chances. It might be really leaving home, letting go of Mom's hand or Dad's, to shoulder the burdens and know the satisfactions of adult living. All these decisions entail dying a death, which frightens us. It is so much easier to cling, even when *that* is killing us. The death and resurrection paradigm, which names the spiritual dimension of this experience, is an enormous support. A man, fifty-nine, writes:

> I made my first real friend in life when I was in my early twenties. It almost killed me to do it. I had been the perfect kid. Everybody respected me because outwardly I did everything well. Inside, I was something else altogether, full of doubts and fears and conflicts. I knew people respected me, but I wondered if anyone could love me if they knew who I really was. I didn't think so, so I always hid. Finally I couldn't stand holding it all in anymore. I was sick and tired of the loneliness and the hypocrisy. One night I dared to tell a guy I hung around with what was really going on inside me. I felt terribly exposed, weak, ashamed; he could have crushed me. Instead, he told me how good it felt to know me as a real human being, and how much it meant to him that I had trusted him. We became close friends. For me, that night was a real death. And I rose to a different life altogether.

In life's longer arduous passages, as, for example, after a divorce, "Holy Saturday" can be a useful metaphor for interpreting the shadowy time in which we often find ourselves between death and new life. Holy Saturday is that formless day between the Friday on which Jesus dies and the Sunday on which he is raised. In the annual reliving of these events in religious celebration, Holy Saturday is a kind of gray, vague, empty day on which nothing happens and one wonders what to feel or do. The acute pain of tragic death has abated somewhat, but nothing new yet stirs. In our lives too, it is sometimes Holy Saturday, often for more than a day. But the death and resurrection paradigm reminds us that Easter will come.

6. The Spirituality of Marriage Lies Chiefly in Fidelity to the Dialogue.

The German philosopher, Friedrich Nietzsche, once remarked: "Marriage is a long conversation; so marry a friend." Marriage is many things. But it does all turn on the ongoing dialogue that lies at its heart. And this principle asserts that God haunts that dialogue, a Voice within the voices, sending messages the spiritual person wants to hear and heed.

God is where the action is, and in marriage the action is in the dialogue. That is where our mate, among assorted other utterances, calls us regularly to a change of heart. No one knows us as well as our mate does. No one is as much affected by all we do and fail to do. Our mate reflects us back to ourselves, and it is not always a pretty picture. The spiritual person, who wants to grow into a decent human being, listens to that summons because God is in it. God is always interested in our growth, always trying to promote it. Marriage is a crucible for that development. It is one of the better places for God to get at us.

Before I got married, I did not really know how selfish I could be. I did not know how moody I was. I did not know what a poor listener I sometimes am. Nobody was ever close

133

enough or honest enough to tell me. Now, in the crucible of intimacy, I am called to grow, and I know that the Voice in the depths is God's own.

The dialogue is not always the bearer of bad news though. Nobody loves us as much as our mate does, at least in the sense of sticking with us and continuing to put out for us even with all our flaws. And sometimes our mate can be downright affirming. Here too the Voice is heard, the faithful Lover in the background who knows us even better than our mate and loves us, strangely, even more. We need this cheering note for our growth just as much as we need the other. These are, in fact, the two hands of every love, Comfort and Challenge, alternately working on us to make something beautiful. Sometimes we see that beauty in older couples who have, as the saying goes, "worked it out."

Is there anything else we should be doing in the dialogue besides listening for the voice of God? Yes. Sometimes it is our turn to speak. Here, the Letter to the Ephesians gives us the ideal in just five words: "…telling the truth with love…" (Eph 4:15). Anyone who is married knows that this remains quite a challenge.

It is, of course, not only in the marital dialogue that the Voice speaks. It can be heard in many other dialogues as well. Which brings us to our next principle.

7. God Often Appears in Human Form.

All Christians celebrate the appearance of God in human form in Jesus of Nazareth. For many, that is where the idea of divine incarnation begins and ends. But that would mean that God is not usually present in the world, and has no other material expression than Jesus. As we have seen, the whole creation is charged with the grandeur of God; everything is symbol and expression of the divine reality. Human beings, by reason of their complexity, have the greatest capacity to express the mystery of God. Karl Rahner was fond of insisting that every human being, not just Jesus, is a potential, and in some degree actual, self-revelation of God. In other words, what Jesus was most fully, each of us already is in some measure, and could become more. This is just an extrapolation of a foundational biblical notion that we are created "in the image and likeness of God" (Gn 1:26).

So we are always meeting God in the streets of the city. God is revealed to us more expressly in those persons who love us especially—friends, parents, children, spouses, mentors. That God loves us and that we have unique value are facts that we all believe—in a way. But we rarely feel it or truly believe it until some human being incarnates that love, expressing it to us in human words, touch, deeds. Then notional assent to the fact of God's love becomes *real* assent, a knowing that is also deeply felt. Those who really love us are true incarnations or sacraments for us—embodiments of the Invisible in the visible. God often appears in human form. For people whom life has handled roughly, even a single warm personal friendship is in the deepest sense a saving relationship.

> God is love, and the person who abides in love abides in God, and God in him or her. (1 Jn 4:16)

> No one has ever seen God. But if we love one another, God dwells in us, and God's love is brought to perfection in us. (1 Jn 4:12)

8. We Are Neither Naturally Good nor Naturally Evil, but Immensely Malleable and Ultimately Responsible for Our Own Becoming.

The Book of Genesis recounts the story of a sinful choice made by the man and woman in the garden, a choice from which multiple alienations flowed. The story is a wonderful piece of art filled with profound insights. However, some Christian theology has gone beyond its intent and extrapolated from it a doctrine of the total corruption of the human person. Supposedly we have no capacity to choose the good or even to think correctly unless we are redeemed from this "fallen state" of "original sin" by Christ. It is difficult to reconcile a dogma of total corruption and helplessness with our actual experience, either of ourselves or of others. It also seems a very poor place from which to start talking about the spiritual life.

In reaction to this extreme denigration of human nature, other thinkers have insisted on the essential goodness of the human person—unless someone corrupts him or her. This premise makes human evildoing an exception or aberration. This does not square with our experience of ourselves or others either.

The truth seems to lie somewhere in the middle, and the Bible, if you read it all, shows a good sense of this as it tells the story of God's people from generation to generation. The characters in the story actually do much that is good, even exhibit heroism on occasion. At the same time they are wayward. They are tempted by the glamour of evil, wander from the path, even sink into corruption. But they recover from that too. Jesus deals with people as if they have a free choice. He calls them to the good, his invitation enfolding a presumption that they can say yes. Many do.

In creating us, it seems, God creates not so much a person as the raw materials for a person. Our creation continues from birth until death, under the influence of our environment and in virtue of our own free choices. The environment contains shaping elements both constructive and destructive. Environment differs from environment in its proportions of good and evil. It is obviously much more difficult to bring wholeness out of cultures of poverty, racism, gender bias, abuse, or addiction than it is from human settings in which love, opportunity, and good example abound. Whatever our situation, as we mature, we have increasing control over our development, with a growing power of choice over possible reactions to our surroundings, even over what sorts of persons we choose to be with. Each of our choices paves the way for the next, making a similar choice easier, a different kind of choice harder. Both our conditioning and the habits we establish do limit our freedom, but always we are free in some measure and therefore responsible for what we do. Wherever we are, grace, the empowering gift of God's love, is always available to us.

Whatever our context, we seem to find ourselves in a field of conflicting forces: a current pulling us toward evil, a current pulling us toward good. Around us stand models of both. If "original sin" means anything, it denotes the downward pull around us and, sympathetically, inside us. It is the history of human failure rolling down the generations with destructive effect. If "grace" means anything, it names the upward pull inside and around us—the call to conversion, the empowerment, the salve of healing, the surprise of liberation. Both forces are ever operative, and we do our self-creation within their tangled matrix.

This reading of the human situation supplies a corrective for those weighed down with a conviction that they are evil at the core. At the same time, it offers a warning to those who have an exaggerated sense of their goodness, unaware of their "shadow side," their weakness and vulnerability to the lure of evil. Examples abound of how, placed in conducive circumstances, anyone of whatever previous condition somehow becomes an embezzler, a betrayer, an abuser, a murderer. The reverse is also the case: "sinners" become "saints." The principle reminds us of our plasticity, and of the responsibility we carry for our own becoming. "The devil made me do it" is a poor excuse. "A person with my past hasn't got a chance" is no alibi either. Always we have a choice. Sometimes the crucial choice is simply asking for help.

9. God's Will for Us Is Found within Our Own Deepest Wanting.

This is a principle for those who seek to do God's will in the important decisions of their lives, but wonder how to discern what God's will is. It indicates where to look. It has just one presupposition: that one's life is generally oriented toward God, or in other words, that one's fundamental intention in life, though always imperfectly executed, is to live in harmony with God's values and purposes.

Then, when we have found what we most deeply want, we have found what God wants for us. This follows simply from God's love for us. If God loves us, then surely God wants us to be ourselves, to do what expresses our true selves, to have what is good and brings us genuine satisfaction. Sometimes Christians think what they want and what God wants are opposed, as if God were against them rather than for them.

Is it God's will that I be a priest or marry and have a family? That I stay with my marriage or leave it? That I put my mother in a nursing home or care for her at home?

First, God does not have a will for the details of our lives. God leaves those to us. Remember, it is cocreation. God's stake in the matter is general rather than particular. The prophet Micah puts God's interest this way:

> This is what Yahweh asks of you, only this:
>> To live justly,
>> to love tenderly,
>> and to walk humbly with your God. (Mi 6:8)

Micah here presents God's will in terms of three broad, overarching values. Jesus, as we saw, puts God's will in a single great commandment: love. Yet many Christians conceive of God's will as a very detailed plan for their lives. Then they discover how difficult it is to get their hands on that plan. Both the Hebrew and Greek words in the Bible for God's will mean "God's yearning,"[4] a term much more suggestive of broad purpose than of specific directions. God presents us with a set of *values* according to which to order our lives, leaving the particular decisions to us. There is no elaborate pre-plan. For this reason, philosopher/theologian Alfred North Whitehead thought it more accurate to substitute the expression God's *purpose* for God's will.[5] Seeking God's will, then, means aligning ourselves with God's purpose and making our specific determinations accordingly.

Faced with an important decision, people often pray and then look for signs, or wait for God to speak some words to them. Well, it is good to pray, the better to align ourselves with God's purpose. But the place to look for the "signs" or "words" is deep within ourselves. When we have found what we most deeply want, we have found what we are seeking. God's purposes for us are planted within our being. God wants our true selfhood to unfold. In speaking here of our deepest wanting, I am obviously not talking about sudden impulse or passing whim, but about a wanting that is persistent and includes both reason and emotion.[6]

Carl Jung frequently urges this same basic idea, though in a different conceptual framework. He stresses the importance of following our destiny, which he says flows out of our inner being. It is only in fidelity to this that we can find the meaning of our life and our true fulfillment. To find our life direction, Jung urges listening always to our deepest self as it speaks in our nocturnal dreams, our day dreams, and our visceral feelings of attraction or repulsion, of consonance or dissonance. It is the same basic insight. The seeds of our destiny, or God's purpose for us, are planted within us.

10. Good People Are in Danger of Being Destroyed by Their Own Goodness.

This was one of the great discoveries of St. Ignatius Loyola. He detected a difference in the patterns of temptation he experienced at various points in his spiritual development. When he observed the same phenomenon many times in the lives of people he guided, he put his insight in writing. Those whose lives are headed in a bad direction are tempted by gross evil: dishonest paths to wealth, quick vengeance when offended, sensual pleasures that hurt other people. Those whose lives are oriented toward God do not find such prospects alluring. They are tempted instead by what seems morally or spiritually good.[7]

For example, they think they should devote even more time to prayer than they already are, or be even more self-effacing, or impose an even stricter fast on themselves, or work even more hours in the service of others. If they are seduced by these apparent calls to a greater holiness, they are eventually destroyed by their own goodness, which is why Ignatius called these attractions temptations. Good people are very subject to them, because they seem like promptings of the Holy Spirit.

The key indicators for discerning which attractions are actually from God are whether they produce true inner peace, and whether in practice they produce the long-range good. Sometimes we must actually try them to find out. Over time, the spiritual person develops an ever keener sense of whether a given course of action feels consonant or dissonant with one's orientation toward God. Ignatius put a lot of stock in that inner-felt sense. He also stressed that the long-range good is the greater good. Good and zealous persons will often exhaust themselves doing some good work. They need counsel to pace themselves, to take care of themselves (to them it seems selfish), because the journey is long. They will do far more good over the long haul than they will if they burn out.

Often we need the help of a spiritually mature person in judging whether what we are doing or considering doing is really good. None of us is a very good judge in our own case. It is not only in matters of religious observance, but also in practical matters of daily life that we can be led astray. We can easily be overresponsible for others, willing to be taken advantage of, unable to say no, or burdened in spirit by the suffering of the world. We think we *must* suffer what we suffer, *must* do what we do; it seems to us a moral or spiritual imperative. We often need assistance in finding a truer sense both of our personal limitations and of what God is really asking. A woman, forty-three, writes:

I used to think about all the suffering people were under-going around the world, especially people in poor coun-tries. It seemed wrong to me to be happy in my own life when all this was going on. How could I not care? It col-ored everything, because every morning I woke up to the same suffering world. It took a spiritual guide to help me see that what I was doing was not good, even though I did it because of love. It was depressing me, and as a result I wasn't a very good wife or mother to those I really could love. I was trying to be God and take care of the whole world, instead of simply praying for everyone and giving the world back to God. I think it came from my childhood, where I was always trying to save my whole dysfunctional family.

Yes. It is good people who are tempted in these ways. And it is very hard, unassisted, to recognize what is going on.

I close with a summary list. And I remember with the deep-est gratitude the persons who over the years have helped me to discover these truths.

1. God wants life for us.
2. The purpose of our life is to learn how to love.
3. Where the action in our life is, God is present and active.
4. God does not send us pain and suffering, but works with us in them for good.
5. The paradigm of death and resurrection is key to understanding our existence.
6. The spirituality of marriage lies chiefly in fidelity to the dialogue.
7. God often appears in human form.
8. We are neither naturally good nor naturally evil, but

immensely malleable and ultimately responsible for our own becoming.

9. God's will for us is found within our own deepest wanting.

10. Good people are in danger of being destroyed by their own goodness.

Questions and Exercises

1. Which of these ten principles strike you as particularly true or helpful, and why? Are there any of the principles you disagree with?

2. When you are trying to figure out what God's will is for your life, either in general or in a particular choice, how do you go about it?

3. Call to mind something you are struggling with in your life right now. Do any of these principles shed any helpful light on it?

4. Look back over some of the main sufferings you have had in your life. Can you see any ways God has worked with you to bring good out of them? In retrospect, are these sufferings a curse or a blessing?

5. Is there anyone in your acquaintance whom you see being destroyed by their own goodness? Have you ever found it happening to you?

6. Can you relate personally to the idea that sometimes we have to die a death in order to come to new life?

7. The chapter is titled "Toward a Life-Giving *Christian* Spirituality." Could it just as well have been called "Toward a Life-Giving Spirituality," or is Jesus somehow significant in what is set forth here?

Chapter Eight

Spirituality and Sexuality

> Sexuality is that part of us through which we reach out to other persons and to God, expressing the need for relationship, for the sharing of self and of meaning.
>
> —*Judith Plaskow*

We exist in the world as sexual beings. There is no other way to be. We are aware of ourselves as male or female, and aware of others as gendered also. There is an energy in this that colors all our relating, sometimes very powerfully. Even if we are celibate, these facts are always operative. Sexuality is much bigger than sex.

We are fascinated by sexuality even as little children. The fascination only grows in adolescence, and it abides through our adult lives. Sexuality is mysterious. It is beautiful. It is compelling. Because of its sweep and power, it can also be a little frightening. One way or another, it is always in our awareness.

What are we to make of this dimension of our existence? What does it mean, and what is it for? And since our chief interest in this book is spirituality, what, if anything, does sexuality have to do with spirituality? In the popular Christian mind, sexuality and spirituality are a world apart. Flesh and spirit are opposites, right? Those who would rise spiritually must leave the flesh and its cravings behind, no?

In this chapter, I am going to claim the very opposite. Sexuality is *suffused* with spirituality; it is *charged* with the Mystery. To see this, let us first develop a general sense of what sexuality means in human life. Then let us explore its suffusion with the spiritual. Finally, let us see if we can develop any moral/spiritual norms for our sexual relating.

Our Essential Need for Relationship

We are essentially relational beings. The word *individual* is an anomaly because, although each of us is in a true sense distinct and autonomous, we cannot live except in connectedness with everything around us. Daily we depend on water, plants, and even animals to supply us with the fuel we live on. We cannot survive for three minutes without a fresh infusion of air. And that is just the beginning. We depend on other people for more goods and services than we can name. And without love, we perish. Nor are human beings alone in their interdependence. The entire cosmos, as we saw, is an *organism*. All is interdependence: mutual need and mutual influence. Within that organism, as a vivid cell, we live and move and have our being.

Our sexuality is one of the ways our hunger for connection comes home to us as a daily experience.[1] It makes restlessly palpable our essential incompleteness. We can see it in our bodies and feel it in our souls. Our sexuality is curiosity, fascination, appreciation, attraction as we take a look around us and notice what is there. It is longing. And when we connect, it is joy.

Physically, sexuality is one of the experiences of our sensuality. Our bodies endow us with a rich capacity for sensual pleasure. We enjoy food and drink through taste, good music by hearing, hugs with our whole body. Our eyes delight in beautiful sights, in nature and in art. Our skin rejoices in the sun's warm touch and the breeze's coolness, in comforting massage, in gentle repose. Sexual pleasure is one of the entrees at this rich smorgasbord of sense pleasure, all God's gifts. It is in good company.

But, like the rest of these joys of human life, our sexual experience is more than merely physical. It may be rooted in our bodiliness, but that is exactly where our spirituality also resides.[2] We are incarnate spirit, and as such are one person, indivisible. Even in our most spiritual activities, our bodies are involved. In our most bodily activities, our spirits are involved. Teilhard de Chardin was fond of putting it this way as he gazed at the world: Matter is the without, spirit the within of things.

Historically, we have been led into misunderstanding and problems when dualistic thinking has broken up this unified vision of matter/spirit. Two of these dualisms have been commonly enough sanctioned by certain versions of spirituality. The first dualism is the split between spirit and body, where spirit is exalted as valuable, body denigrated as valueless and even inimical to the spiritual life. The second dualism is the split between male and female, where maleness is exalted and made normative, femaleness designated as second best, subordinate, and even suspect. The third dualism presents itself under the banner of the sexual revolution of modern times. Sexual gratification is there split off from genuine human personhood and becomes an end in itself, without respect for persons or for fully human relating.

If we can steer clear of these dualisms and maintain a unified vision, we can celebrate our sexuality as one of the more wonderful signs of our vitality, a gift of God fecund and filled with promise—even if we have to be careful to manage it responsibly lest it cause harm.

Sexuality and Spirituality

A man in his fifties answered thus when I asked him what he seeks spiritually at this time in his life:

> I seek to know intimately the experience of spirituality within sexuality.

What an enlightened quest! He was one of the few to bring sexuality into the questionnaire on spirituality at all. What he seeks is worth seeking. And the news is good, for the mystery of sexuality is indeed *charged* with the mystery of God. Sexuality is diaphanous; the light of God shines through it. This intimate link with the Divine is the secret of its immense power over us. Wherever we experience that kind of power, we should suspect the divine presence. Yet somehow this tremendous primal recognition has gone almost entirely unacknowledged, certainly uncelebrated, in church teaching.[3]

On what basis do I assert this suffusion of sexuality with Spirit? It is part of a bigger picture, with which we have already become familiar. We always find the Spirit *in* the flesh, in matter. We can only find it there because we live in the world and are ourselves body persons. Our communication with other humans, spirit to spirit, can only be accomplished through the flesh. Sexual expression is one of its many modes. Our communication with God is in exactly the same case. We find God in the world, in matter. God is the Soul of the world, and all of nature theophany. In Jesus, God appears resplendently in the flesh—where else? What the spiritual person tries to do is not to shun matter, but to recognize and draw out of it more of what it always houses and expresses: Spirit.

We noted previously that particularly where we encounter depth, mystery, power, our attention is caught and we know that we are in contact with something more, the Mystery. Well, is there any more compelling instance of depth, mystery, power for us as human beings than our sexuality?

Consider. Sexuality runs all through the plant, animal, and human realms, a core dimension, plainly, of God's grand design. Do you like flowers? Flowers are the sex organs of plants. In the human realm even more, sexuality is charged with the mystery of God. One of the books of the Bible, the Song of Songs, sees this clearly, and in a long poem celebrates erotic love in all its aspects. Here are a couple of passages.

> My beloved is a sachet of myrrh
> lying between my breasts.
> My beloved is a cluster of henna flowers
> among the vines of Engedi.
>
> How beautiful you are, my beloved,
> and how delightful!
> All green is our bed. (Sg 1:13–16)
>
> How beautiful are your feet in their sandals,
> O prince's daughter!
> The curve of your thighs is like the curve of a necklace,
> work of a master hand.
> Your navel is a bowl well rounded
> with no lack of wine,

your belly a heap of wheat
surrounded with lilies.
Your two breasts are two fawns
twins of a gazelle. (Sg 7:2–5)

This sacred poetry, full of wonder and joy, simply calls attention to what we ourselves have felt. A man, sixty, answering my question, "Have you ever had a religious experience?" speaks for many when he writes:

Yes. The first time I made love after years of celibacy. I felt very close to God, nature, and to the woman I loved. It was a fantastic experience.

The Book of Genesis takes us all the way back to creation, expressing the same wonder and sense of gift as it narrates:

Then the Lord God said, "It is not good that the man should be alone; I will make him a helper as his partner...." So the Lord God caused a deep sleep to fall upon the man, and he slept; then he took one of his ribs and closed up its place with flesh. And the rib that the Lord God had taken from the man he made into a woman and brought her to the man. Then the man said:

"This at last is bone of my bones,
    and flesh of my flesh;
  this one shall be called Woman,
    for out of Man this one was taken."

Therefore a man leaves his father and his mother and clings to his wife, and they become one flesh. And the man and his wife were both naked, and were not ashamed. (Gn 2:18–25 NRSV).

How primal what this poetry describes. No wonder sexuality holds such sway over us; it is of God through and through. We are fascinated by sexuality and romance. Why do you suppose advertisers appeal to it so much when they want us to buy something? We long for sexual/romantic connection, fantasize about it, eat our hearts out if we do not have it, go to great lengths to get it. Yet seldom is the obvious connection between this human mystery and the Great Mystery called attention to. But surely our longing for an intimate human partner is intertwined with our even deeper longing for God. That human partner is what we want, and at the same time is only a symbol of what we *really* want.

Nor is it only through longing that we contact God here. When we experience the beauty of our own and others' bodies and personalities, the power of sexual attraction, and the profound pleasure of sexual relating itself, we know that we are enjoying a great and marvelous gift. And it is not just a gift from one Person to another, as if God said: "Here, you can have this." The divine mystery expresses something of *Itself* in all of this in a way that stirs us profoundly. A beautiful sunset, it has long been held, is apt matter for the contemplation of the divine. Is sexuality any less so? Is it any less filled with beauty, goodness, and mystery? Where the works of God's hands are concerned, I doubt that I am alone in finding sexuality right up there with the sunset.

A woman who had been married for a long time once remarked to me in counseling:

> This is what I would like for the next phase of our marriage—that our sexual relating become more spiritual. I want it to be more than just the same old physical ritual one more time; not just hands, but hands and heart and

soul. I want to give and to feel the deep and many-sided love we have gradually developed through the years. I believe that if we can really make love person to person, we will find more of God in it too.

I realized when I heard this that it was what I wanted in my own marriage. And although I am not sure, life being what it is, that we or any other couple can achieve this kind of communication every time we make love, it certainly seems worth striving for.

Moral/Spiritual Norms for Our Sexual Relating

The spiritual person is, of course, keenly interested in the contemplative dimension of the mystery of sexuality. But he or she also wants very much to do what is good in sexual relating. Let us go on to explore how good and evil in sexual relating are to be discerned.

We might begin by asking what Jesus has to say about this. As we saw in an earlier chapter, he gives us little in the way of a sexual ethic. Nor, for that matter, do the Hebrew scriptures, which lie behind him. Recall what has been written earlier: Jesus says nothing at all about masturbation, premarital sex, homosexuality. Nor does he extol celibacy, as if the whole topic of sexuality were unworthy of spiritual consideration. It is at a wedding, in fact, that he chooses to perform one of his most lavish signs, the changing of an immense amount of water (180 gallons) into wine for the celebration. He does take a clear position against adultery and for marital permanence. And he speaks against a man's lusting after a woman in his heart (this just a single line and appearing in only one of the gospels,

Mt 5:28). Here he calls men on our tendency to make women mere sexual objects, encouraging us to reverence women as persons with their own dignity and their own lives.

While he offers little sexual instruction, Jesus does speak to the issue in exhibiting an immense concern for the quality of human relationships. It is here that he gives us the norm we seek. It is a moral/spiritual ideal. His single, overarching principle for all of our relating is genuine human love. What implications does this norm have for sexual relationships?[4]

One way to see a matter clearly is to start from the opposite side. It is clear that sex can hurt people. It hurts people when it is violent or abusive, when it seeks self-gratification without regard for the feelings or well-being of the other person. This is exactly the opposite of love. The two worst cases of it are taking sexual advantage of a child for one's own gratification, and rape. Both are traumatic events for the victim, profoundly damaging, very difficult to heal. But sexual exploitation has other forms too: the man ever on the sexual hunt who leads women on, the man who forces sex on his partner against her wishes, the man so bent on his own pleasure that he has little regard for his partner's pleasure or pain, the man who acts considerately toward his mate only when he wants sex from her, the man who sexually harasses women.

These are acts of violence, abuses of power, the stronger taking advantage of the weaker. They can occur just as easily in marriage as outside it. There is also a passive-aggressive use of power in the sexual realm, which can be exercised by either party in a committed relationship. That is sexual withholding, used as punishment or manipulation. I do not mean to suggest that a person must always say yes to a sexual overture. There are often good reasons for saying no. I am speaking of a stance, a deliberate use of sex as power, this time in the form of a total or consistent refusal. It is a strong one-up position, which, like active aggression, really hurts the other person and the relationship. What love would suggest is that the sexual realm not be used as a power realm at all. A couple caught up in this hurtful kind of power game need to face the deeper issues they are in conflict over. Then they can give the sexual realm the protection it deserves for the expression of their love.

Two norms suggest themselves for breaking the love commandment down for clearer application to sexual relating: *authenticity* and *responsibility*. *Authenticity* means being honest, a challenging ideal in sexual relating, where it is so easy to pretend in order to get what one wants. *Responsibility* means being careful, soberly assessing consequences and being genuinely concerned for the welfare of one's mate, oneself, and any life that may result from sexual relating. Being honest and being care-ful rule out sexuality's most common abuses: promiscuity, exploitation, careless pregnancy, and the transmission of disease. All of these obviously hurt other people and ourselves as well, and hence violate the love commandment.

Those who would love truly need to keep their communication open as they keep testing their developing sexual relationship for authenticity and responsibility. It is not uncommon in a developing love relationship for sex to start early and soon lead the way, so that when the couple is together, they are sharing physical intimacies much more than really getting to know one another or talking about issues they need to talk about. This is inauthentic, because all the physical tenderness being expressed is way ahead of the actual bond between the two. Let an unexpected pregnancy occur and the couple quickly realize how weak their foundations are and how completely unprepared they are to make a life together in support of this child. Even short of pregnancy, if we listen closely to our own hearts and hear our mate out through dialogue, we will often enough find that one or the other of us is not entirely comfortable with the way our sexual intimacy fits into the larger picture of this relationship and our lives as a whole.

Teenage sexuality is a separate issue. It is not the same as adult sexuality, and so a different norm applies. Sexual relating demands emotional maturity and good judgment. Without them, people get hurt. As a society we have enshrined the difference between the teenager and the adult in at least three basic laws. No one can drive a car until they are sixteen. No one can vote until they are eighteen or twenty-one. No one can buy alcohol until they are twenty-one. Why these laws? Because there are some things it is just not wise to get into until one has achieved the necessary maturity. They are too powerful, and are fraught with danger.

Teenagers do not yet possess the necessary emotional maturity and judgment to take on the emotional weight and all the complexities of sexual relating. And so a different standard applies to them than applies to adults. In the teen years, celibacy is not some uptight, unreasoning adult prohibition, but pretty plainly the wiser course. Choosing the alternative constitutes playing with fire, and too many have been burned. This is, of course, a hard sell for parents trying to reach their teenage children. What red-blooded teenager wants to hear the message: Sex is a great and wonderful thing, but you are not ready yet? The dialogue is taxing, but what a crucial area for engagement and ongoing discussion. It is right up there with the biggies: how to manage that car responsibly, how to use alcohol moderately, how to be a contributing citizen. This one gets quite personal, too. Parents will probably have to admit to their kids that they, too, are sexual beings, that they have struggled with this in their own lives, that they have made mistakes, that they have learned some things the hard way and would like to spare their kids the pain.

We owe our children plenty of dialogue around sexuality. We owe them a positive presentation of its goodness and spiritual significance. They need good sex education. They need a thorough exploration of all the emotional and ethical issues involved in sexual relating. And if we can learn a lesson from the experience of the churches where trying to hold the line is concerned, it will not be enough in dealing with our kids just to say no. We will have to give reasons and examples that persuade.

Sex is a great and wonderful gift. It is a window into the Mystery. It stirs joy, gratitude, and awe. It also has a moral dimension. Our sexuality is given to us as a powerful relational force. It needs to be tamed, humanized, spiritualized. If learning to love is the highest value in the Christian spiritual life, then learning to integrate our sexuality into genuine loving is a matter of the greatest concern to anyone wishing to grow personally and spiritually. The challenge is sufficient to occupy us for a lifetime.

Questions and Exercises

1. Does your sexual experience support the chapter's claims that sexuality is charged with the Holy and that sexual experience is also somehow an experience of the Mystery? How?

2. Have you ever felt the need for moral norms in your own exercise of sexuality? What norms have you used? How do your norms compare to the norms proposed here: the law of love, further broken down into concern for authenticity and responsibility?

3. How does the presentation of sexuality in this chapter compare to what you may have been exposed to in a church, synagogue, mosque, or temple?

4. A mature and spiritually serious man of my acquaintance once remarked: "My sexuality *is* my spirituality, and my spirituality is my sexuality." He made me think. How do you react to his statement?

5. Choose two TV programs, two movies, or three advertisements. What are they saying about human sexuality?

Chapter Nine

The Movement of the Spirit and the Challenge to the Churches

The temple bell stops
But the sound keeps coming out of the flowers.
—*Basho*

We have surveyed a lot of spirituality without saying much about the churches. Yet most of us grew up in a church and probably regarded it as the chief source and support of our spiritual life. In the last thirty years, membership in the mainline Christian churches has dropped significantly. Yet spiritual interest is keen. What is the problem?

The Barna Research Group of California recently made a survey of the unchurched, asking a simple question: "Why don't you go to church?" Seventy-four percent said they don't because they see no value in it; they can connect with God more easily in other contexts. Sixty-one percent gave a second reason: The churches have too many problems. Forty-eight percent said they simply don't have time; Sundays are their only day to relax. Forty percent were bothered by the churches being too money oriented. Only twelve percent said they did not attend because they do not believe in God.[1]

The issue of church remains an important one for spiritual pilgrims today, even if it is a difficult one to resolve. They neither wish to go it alone, nor would they long survive without the support and input of some community of fellow seekers. Many would like to belong to a church, yet have difficulty finding one they would like to belong to. Others cling to the church of their childhood, though dissatisfied. They hang on partly in hope that change will come soon, partly from such a deep and long-standing love with their familiar church and its people that they cannot quite tear themselves away, though their current needs are very poorly met there. Two women express this very typical quandary well. One searches for a suitable church; one still attends the church of her childhood, but tenuously.

> I've not found a church where I feel I "belong." One that has a theology I resonate with and that has a range of persons—age and ethnic diversity. I want a mission, a building, and a people to invest myself in. And I don't want to drive an hour to get there.

> Why do I stay? Because it is my grounding. Because I crave a community (although I have not found it yet). Because I can't yet accept grace enough to be unchurched and believing. Because I love to sing. Because I need hugs.

To my mind, the outpouring of spiritual vitality among us today constitutes an immense opportunity for the institutional churches. It also deeply challenges them. In this final chapter, I would like to survey all the wonderful movements, both inside and outside the churches, that demonstrate how the Spirit is breathing among us in fresh, creative ways. Then I would like to sketch a dream.

Fresh Winds

1. *Liberation movements.* In many lands all around the world, the Spirit is stirring and empowering people to demand their liberation from oppression. The movement began in Latin America in the 1960s, and generated a whole new understanding of what it means to be a Christian. Theology set out from a new starting point—the experience of poor and oppressed people. Reading the scriptures with fresh eyes, it discovered how deep and pervasive in the biblical tradition is the experience of God as *Liberator* from all oppressions. The Hebrews first became a people when Yahweh freed them from slavery in Egypt and gave them their own land. Liberation continued through the generations with the consistent denunciations by Yahweh's prophets of social injustice as it sprang up again and again in Hebrew and Jewish society. It came to forceful focus again in Jesus' messianic ministry. He so clearly championed the cause of the poor and marginalized, fearlessly confronting abuses of power and wealth. To be a follower of his clearly meant struggling for liberation from all oppressions, both for oneself and for others. From Latin America, liberation theology spread to Africa, which began creating a theology apt for its own situation. Now the movement is growing in Asia as well. These manifestations of the Spirit call those of us who enjoy wealth and power in the West to a radical change of heart, to a much broader conception of what Christian love demands in today's world. Meanwhile, in the West, too, internal liberation movements have sprung up. The drive for racial equality, for an end to discrimination against gay and lesbian persons, for the full equality of women, and for democratic structures in the church are vibrant examples.

2. *The women's movement.* This manifestation of the Spirit deserves special elaboration because of its singular fruitfulness and widespread implications. Discrimination against women has existed in practically every society in the world and still does. Besides the immense suffering it has caused women, the price tag is a tremendous loss to the human community of women's thinking, experience, and gifts. Think of the lives in which countless women have been and still are confined, denied the opportunity to develop their talents, confined to narrow spheres of activity assigned them by men, their ideas dismissed, their spirits often further crushed by verbal, sexual, and physical abuse. No wonder there is a liberation movement all across the world. With tremendous energy and perseverance, women are pushing their way into more and more spheres of social life. They are finding and sharing their theological perspectives, immensely enriching the churches. They are changing the way we think about God, power, social arrangements, our relationship to earth. They stand in solidarity with all other liberation movements, calling for a respect and mutuality that must pervade all the relationships in the great web of creation. There is enough fresh thought and energy here to change the world. Veteran theologian Marcus Borg, a prominent figure in the Jesus Seminar, calls the emergence of feminist theology "the single most important development in theology in my lifetime."[2]

3. *The base community movement.* The base, or small, community movement started in Latin America about the same time liberation theology did. The two developments stimulated and supported one another. People organized themselves into small groups to study scripture together, to see what it had to say to their life situation. As they learned, they began strategizing and pooling their resources to bring about the social changes that

scripture demanded. The result was a tremendous revitalization of church and social life—a vision and a push that soon became threatening both to civil and to church authorities. The base community movement has remained strong in spite of persecution and has spread across the world in a variety of forms.[3] What it has meant to typical parish life is that people lost in the large anonymous congregation are known by name and feel a true sense of belonging in a group of manageable size. These subgroups have their own specific learning and social change objectives, and satisfy the hunger for genuine community and focused purpose.

4. *The ecumenical movement and the dialogue of world religions.* The ecumenical movement promotes dialogue among Christian denominations at both popular and scholarly levels, in order to heal divisions, find theological consensus on disputed points, pray and worship together, and collaborate on projects for the good of humanity.[4] The dialogue of world religions extends this exchange and collaboration further still, reaching across the globe to bring representatives of the major religions together in order to promote mutual understanding, find common ground, stimulate each other to growth, and work together on projects to improve life for everyone. The feeling is growing among people everywhere that the world can no longer afford religious divisions and conflicts; that what we all seek through participation in religion are the same worthy things; and that all the good will, energy, and resources that exist in religious people of all persuasions need to be channeled into a common effort to save the world.

5. *Fresh theological insight and understanding.* Christian theology is fully awake and engrossed with the issues of the day, teeming with fresh insight for the enrichment of the spiritual life. The churches have assimilated and proclaimed but a frac-

tion of it. In Roman Catholic circles ever since the 1960s, when the Second Vatican Council invited theologians to present the core convictions of the tradition in language suited to the contemporary situation and its diverse cultures, an immense amount of creative work has been done to refurbish the understandings that are core to being a Christian. Many threads have contributed to a rich tapestry of theological reformulation: new approaches to the study of scripture, a developing sense of the time-and-culture-bound nature of any formulation of truth, the dialogue of the religions, the increased participation of women, the inclusion of whole peoples scarcely represented before in the work of theology, new knowledge coming from many disciplines, and tough questions and challenges arising from the contemporary situation. What has been achieved is well known among the theologically educated. It has yet to flow into the mainstream of the church's life.

6. *A strong ecological concern for all things, living and nonliving.* The rapid growth of the world's human population and the application of modern technologies to nature have brought the planet to a serious crisis. Air and water are polluted, vast forests have been destroyed, other natural resources are being used up as if there were no tomorrow, many plant and animal species are in danger of extinction, and the specter of nuclear annihilation still hangs over the earth. People are waking up to the gravity of the situation. Our own survival is at stake. And there is so much more that is precious to us in the world that we simply cannot allow the depredation to continue. Theology supports our instinctive love with a sense of the sacredness of earth. The energy is there both to educate and to push for legislation to enjoin a more temperate and reverential interaction with the delicately balanced, sensitive organism we call the universe.

7. *The growth of lay ministry.* The sharp distinction between clergy and laity is breaking down as ordinary people step forward to take more responsibility for the life of the church. Their sense of vocation is well grounded, as Jesus calls *all* his followers, not just a special elite, to ministry, which is simply the Latin word for service, service to the needs of the human community. In the Roman Catholic church, there have never been nearly so many lay people in the ministries of parish and diocese. But this ministry of the laity is much broader than church work. What it labors for is the transformation of all dimensions of human life—social, political, and economic as well as religious. It seeks liberation from all the oppressions which now prevail, so that the world may be brought into conformity with God's gracious purpose.

8. *The emergence of four deep hungers: hunger for ritual, for personal prayer, for community, and for collaborative leadership.* Appetite signals ripeness, a need and a readiness to receive. Those who have left their churches in dissatisfaction often say that what they miss the most is the *ritual*, the expression in symbolic action of realities beyond words. Ritual speaks to deeply felt human needs. And so people today, especially women, are creating their own: rituals for rites of passage in life, for supportive prayer and a laying on of hands in trying times, for the celebration of gifts received and victories won, for the cleansing of neighborhoods, for the invocation of God's support in challenging personal and community endeavors, and for the general spiritual maintenance and growth of their communities.

The *hunger for personal prayer* is evidenced in the flocking to workshops on meditation and the popularity of books on the subject. People want something more than the simple prayers they learned to say as children. They seek what monasticism has provided for small numbers of reclusive Christians—a way of becoming quiet and getting into personal contact with the Mystery. They want to know how to ground and center their lives. They long for inner peace and a more focused approach to all they do.

The *hunger for community* is seen in the proliferation of groups gathering for various ends: AA groups and all their off-shoots, Bible study groups, prayer groups, women's support groups, men's groups, therapy groups. In his *Sharing the Journey: Support Groups and America's New Quest for Community*, Robert Wuthnow tells us that nationally, some 44 percent of women and 36 percent of men are currently members of small groups, which meet regularly and provide caring and support for their members.[5] This manifest need for community used to be met partly by the churches; in some places it still is. The new suburban megachurches, despite their size, are wisely careful to address this need to belong by providing a host of special-interest groups under the big tent. There is something for everyone—a group where people know you and your story, and are dealing with what you are concerned about. In a society in which the extended family is scattered and the neighborhood is usually anonymous, those who search for a group to belong to really appreciate it when trustworthy organizations like the church lead the way in providing for their needs.

The *hunger for collaborative leadership*. In today's climate, authority from on high neither impresses nor persuades. Hierarchical models of leadership are increasingly resisted, as decisions made at that level are so often out of touch with people's real needs, questions, and concerns. Particularly where the general level of education is high and where democratic models of governance have been operative, people are unwilling either simply to believe what authority proclaims as true or to follow orders without question. Still more so in a church community, where the Spirit breathes in all the members and personal gifts meant for the life of the whole community are generously scattered, it makes no sense for power to reside in the hands of a few. The women's movement has been richly generative of models for mutuality and collaboration in leadership.[6] There is fulsome promise here for much richer life in the church.

The Challenge to the Institutional Churches

The sum of these developments constitutes a tremendous challenge to the churches. It is also a wonderful opportunity. The challenge lies in the fact that if the churches embrace all that the Spirit is doing and welcome it into their life, a major accommodation would be required: the revamping of traditional theologies, the reform of structures of authority and ministry, the rechanneling of monies and energies away from what does not meet people's needs into what does, the positive encouragement of semiautonomous base communities within the larger community, the revitalization of ritual, and a rededication to building the reign of God both in the church and in the world. What is demanded is obviously quite a change of heart. The opportunity lies in the fact that by thus losing its life, the institutional church would save it. Immediately it would enjoy greatly increased membership and vitality.

The challenge is daunting. But consider the anomaly. It is to *our own institutional churches* that all of us who pulsate to this spiritual resurgence are looking. It is as if we are reminding them: Look, we are your people! This is your Spirit! Look at this array of wonderful movements. You can have all this. In fact, you originated some of it. You can celebrate all this growth and go through the exhilaration of working with us to fashion new forms and structures for the support and continuance of all this efflorescence. What could be more exciting or worthwhile? It is filled with life for the world. True, in the process you must be transformed, and transformation has its pains. But you need all these new developments for your own life and growth. And you have so much in your storehouse of accumulated wisdom to give to them—to us! We need you. We want you. You need us too.

To focus for just a moment on one aspect of this prospective transformation, it would call for a new kind of church leader and a new conception of ministry. Take the Roman Catholic Church, for example. In a recent article in *America* magazine, a parish priest, reflecting on the present state of affairs, asserts that we need a different kind of priest today than the kind Catholics grew up with. That priest was a "man of the sacraments," who, in a secular world, lived apart and made God present for the rest of us in a sacred space through sacred rituals. Many priests still see that as their life and role. But today, this writer points out, the situation is drastically changed. We see the "secular" world as basically good and already filled with the presence of God. What we want from our spiritual leaders is guidance and inspiration for our relationship with God in the world. He writes:

> I think a priesthood that shares the search and participates in the journey is vital for our religious imagination....Life defined as an open-ended search is at the core of the contemporary experience. We need a priestly ministry that participates in the search, knows revelation and tradition well enough to know when we are off the path and can celebrate the whole: the doubts, struggles, the insights, and the occasional right moves. We also need a prophetic ministry that can challenge the idols of the contemporary scene.[7]

His is an appealing vision of the new priest as spiritual guide—an earnest seeker who is also solidly grounded in the tradition; a perpetual student whose vision keeps deepening and expanding; on both counts, a person with wealth to share with fellow travelers. Sacred rituals would continue to play an important role in the life of the community led by such a priest. But equal time and attention would be poured into guidance, teaching, and personal inspiration in the open-ended spiritual quest.

In Summary

The spiritual quest is alive and well in America and around the world. At the same time, paradoxically, the mainline churches are in a bit of a crisis. They have not caught up with all that the Spirit is doing among the people, and there is tension between the institution and its present and former members. This book has been written out of two cardinal convictions:

1. There is so much that is valuable in the Christian tradition, it would be a great shame for Christians engaged in the new spiritual quest to lose its treasures as they start all over. Even its organizational structures, which need an overhaul, contain items of value.

2. The tradition and the organization really need renewal—a rethinking, an adaptation to changed conditions, and a presentation in which people today will hear an unmistakable ring of relevance and of truth.

I have laid out some of the treasures of the tradition, even as I have also attempted to refurbish them, so that their splendor can shine forth more compellingly. I have focused particularly on God, Jesus, sexuality, and spirituality. These are all crucial areas of consideration for the spiritual pilgrim, and so much good theological work has been done on them in recent years.

The growing divergence between heady spiritual seekers and the churches that formed them need grow no wider. This is a divorce that can be prevented. And it should. There is tremendous growth potential for both parties. Wonderful new things are happening just when it seems everything is falling apart. The poet Gerard Manley Hopkins speaks beautifully of the mystery of regeneration, and names the source of our hope.

> And for all this, nature is never spent;
> There lives the dearest freshness deep down things;
> And though the last lights off the black West went
> Oh, morning, at the brown brink eastward, springs—
> Because the Holy Ghost over the bent
> World broods with warm breast and with ah! bright wings.
> ("God's Grandeur")

Questions and Exercises

1. If you have left the church of your childhood, why have you done so? What have you gained, and what have you lost? Is a return thinkable? If you have stayed, what has held you? And how have you dealt with your church's shortcomings?

2. Have you personally been a part of any of the movements the chapter presents as signs of spiritual vitality today? Are you in a movement *inside* or *outside* your church? Are there other movements you would add to the list?

3. Do you think the integration of all the new spiritual movements into the established churches is possible? Is it desirable? What would happen to each of the parties in the integration?

4. Spend some minutes in quiet prayer and then imagine your local church really embodying the vision of Jesus for the new millennium. Consider membership, leadership, and principal activities of the community. If you can do this as a group excercise, end by sharing your visions.

NOTES

Introduction

1. *New York Times Magazine*, December 7, 1997, 60.

2. An absorbing account of the rapid growth of pentecostalism not only in the United States but around the world is given by Harvey Cox in his *Fire from Heaven: The Rise of Pentecostal Spirituality and the Reshaping of Religion in the Twenty-First Century* (Reading, Mass: Addison-Wesley, 1995). He is also very clear on the differences between pentecostalism and fundamentalism.

3. Karen Armstrong traces the development of that master story in her *A History of God: The 4000-Year Quest of Judaism, Christianity, and Islam* (New York: Ballantine Books, 1993), a deeply informed and very readable account of the spiritual quest in the three great monotheistic religions, from Abraham's time to the present.

4. For a systematic presentation of the basics of the Christian faith in contemporary perspective, see Kathleen Fischer and Thomas Hart, *Christian Foundations: An Introduction to Faith in Our Time*, rev. ed. (Mahwah, N.J.: Paulist Press, 1995).

5. I asked six questions, then elicited demographic information. The questions:

- Have you ever had a religious experience?
- Do you have any experience of God in your ordinary, day-to-day life? If so, when, where, how?
- If you are a churchgoer, what keeps you going there? If you are not, why do you stay away?

- What are the beliefs and hopes that keep you going in life?
- At this point in your life, what do you seek spiritually, or what questions do you have?
- What are two or three of the most important books or articles you've read lately, or movies or plays you've seen, and what was significant about them for you?

Chapter 1. The New Cosmology and the Mystery

1. There are several recent books that detail the new scientific view of the universe and then reflect on its implications for theology. I recommend: Paul Davies, *The Mind of God: The Scientific Basis for a Rational World* (New York: Simon and Schuster, 1992); Kitty Ferguson, *The Fire in the Equations: Science, Religion, and the Search for God* (Grand Rapids, Mich.: Eerdmans, 1994); John F. Haught, *Science and Religion: From Conflict to Conversation* (Mahwah, N.J.: Paulist Press, 1995); Fritjof Capra and David Steindl-Rast, *Belonging to the Universe: Explorations on the Frontiers of Science and Spirituality* (Harper San Francisco, 1991); Danah Zohar, *The Quantum Self: Human Nature and Consciousness Defined by the New Physics* (New York: Quill/William Morrow, 1990); Sallie McFague, *The Body of God: An Ecological Theology* (Minneapolis: Fortress, 1993); Diarmuid O'Murchu, *Quantum Theology: Spiritual Implications of the New Physics* (New York: Crossroad, 1997); Beatrice Bruteau, *God's Ecstasy: The Creation of a Self-Creating World* (New York: Crossroad, 1997).

2. As quoted in Annie Dillard, *Pilgrim at Tinker Creek: A Mystical Excursion into the Natural World* (New York: Bantam, 1974), 96.

3. As quoted in John Davidson, *The Secret of the Creative Vacuum* (London: C. W. Daniel, 1989), 128.

4. Alfred North Whitehead, *Science and the Modern World* (New York: Macmillan, 1953), 36.

5. David S. Toolan, S.J., "At Home in the Cosmos: The Poetics of Matter=Energy," in *America* 174, 6 (Feb. 23, 1996), 14.

6. Alfred North Whitehead, *Science and the Modern World*, vii.

Notes

Chapter 2. God Needs a New Description, a New Location, and a New Name

1. Paul Tillich, *The Shaking of the Foundations* (New York: Scribners, 1948), 57.

2. David S. Toolan, S.J., "At Home in the Cosmos: The Poetics of Matter=Energy," 10.

3. Anthony de Mello, among others, has published collections of such stories from the various wisdom traditions. See, for example, his *The Song of the Bird* (Chicago: Loyola University Press, 1983) and his *Taking Flight* (New York: Doubleday, 1988).

4. Mary Catherine Hilkert develops this point well in a book on preaching, *Naming Grace: Preaching and the Sacramental Imagination* (New York: Continuum, 1997).

5. Marcus Borg, in his *The God We Never Knew* (Harper San Francisco, 1997), 57–83, deftly traces the difference one's operative model for God makes in the living of the Christian life.

6. See, for example, Rosemary Radford Ruether, *Sexism and God-Talk: Toward a Feminist Theology* (Boston: Beacon, 1983); Anne E. Carr, *Transforming Grace: Christian Tradition and Women's Experience* (New York: Harper and Row, 1988); Elizabeth A. Johnson, *She Who Is: The Mystery of God in Feminist Theological Discourse* (New York: Crossroad, 1992); Catherine Mowry LaCugna, ed., *Freeing Theology: The Essentials of Theology in Feminist Perspective* (Harper San Francisco, 1993).

7. Sally McFague, *Models of God* (Minneapolis: Fortress, 1987).

8. Rosemary Radford Ruether, *Disputed Questions: On Being a Christian* (Nashville: Abingdon, 1982), 24.

Chapter 3. What Is "Spirituality"?

1. *SELF*, Dec. 1997, 135.

2. All but Fischer's and Schneiders' statements are quoted from Frederic and Mary Ann Brussat, *Spiritual Literacy: Reading the Sacred in*

Everyday Life (New York: Scribners, 1996), 28–29. Fischer offered her definition in a public lecture in Seattle, March 1989. Schneiders' statement appears in Bradley C. Hanson, ed., *Modern Christian Spirituality* (Atlanta: Scholars Press, 1990), 36.

3. Brussat, *Spiritual Literacy*, 545.

4. Ibid., 28.

5. Rosemary Radford Ruether, *Disputed Questions: On Being a Christian* (Nashville: Abingdon, 1982), 26.

6. Abraham Maslow, influenced in this subject matter by William James, John Dewey, and Rudolph Otto, develops this idea in his *Religions, Values, and Peak-Experiences* (New York: Penguin Books, 1970), 19.

7. Viktor E. Frankl, *Man's Search for Meaning* (New York: Washington Square Press, 1963), 153.

8. C. S. Lewis, *Surprised by Joy* (New York: Collins, 1955), 134.

9. David Steindl-Rast, a Roman Catholic monk active in the Buddhist-Christian dialogue, thinks the Buddhist and I are on very much the same ground. He remarks: "What the Buddhists call *shunyata* (nothing) comes as close as anybody can to speaking about God as horizon. Any Christian who is in dialogue with Buddhists should feel perfectly comfortable accepting *shunyata* as pointing toward God. After all, even the term *God* only points toward God. Of the horizon you never can say, 'There it is.' It's nothing. When you meet Buddhists on this common ground of no-thing, you can talk with them about God. I have experienced that more than once. When Buddhists recognize that you accept *shunyata*, emptiness, nothing, as that horizon which we happen to call God, it clicks." Fritjof Capra and David Steindl-Rast, *Belonging to the Universe: Explorations on the Frontiers of Science and Spirituality* (Harper San Francisco, 1991), 101.

10. For further development of these points, see Richard McBrien, *Catholicism*, rev. ed. (Harper San Francisco, 1994), 1016–21.

Notes

Chapter 4. How Can I Tell If I Am Making Progress in the Spiritual Life?

1. William Johnston, *The Still Point* (New York: Harper and Row, 1970), xiii.

2. As cited by his good friend, columnist Tim Unsworth, in *NCR*, May 8, 1998, 12.

3. Two fine books on Centering Prayer are Thomas Keating, *Open Mind, Open Heart* (New York: Amity House, 1986) and Basil Pennington, *Centering Prayer* (New York: Doubleday, 1982).

4. Anthony de Mello, *Sadhana: A Way to God* (St. Louis: Institute of Jesuit Sources, 1978).

5. Diana Eck, *Encountering God: A Spiritual Journey from Bozeman to Banaras* (Boston: Beacon Press, 1993), 144–65.

6. For a fuller discussion, see Paul Knitter, "Toward a Liberation Theology of Religions" in John Hick and Paul Knitter, eds., *The Myth of Christian Uniqueness* (Maryknoll, N.Y.: Orbis, 1987); and Hans Kung, "What Is True Religion? Toward an Ecumenical Criteriology" in Leonard Swidler, ed., *Toward a Universal Theology of Religion* (Maryknoll, N.Y.: Orbis, 1987).

Chapter 5. Jesus: Trailblazer, Window to the Mystery

1. Christian historian Jaroslav Pelikan has written an interesting account of how the figure of Jesus has been differently but deeply drawn upon by each age from the first century to the twentieth according to its needs. He lays out this collection of portraits in *Jesus through the Centuries: His Place in the History of Culture* (New York: Harper and Row, 1985).

2. What follows is developed more at length in Thomas Hart, *To Know and Follow Jesus* (Mahwah, N.J.: Paulist Press, 1984), 24–40, and again in Kathleen Fischer and Thomas Hart, *Christian Foundations*, rev. ed., 76–94. Albert Nolan's, *Jesus Before Christianity* (Maryknoll, N.Y.:

Orbis, 1976) is a moving account of Jesus' life and teaching before the overlay of Christian dogma, a contemporary reading made in an African setting. Marcus Borg, in my opinion the most balanced and spiritually richest of those writing out of the work of the Jesus Seminar, achieves much the same thing for our own cultural context in his *Jesus: A New Vision* (New York: Harper and Row, 1987), and then more briefly in his *Meeting Jesus Again for the First Time* (Harper San Francisco, 1994). A journalist, Russell Shorto, writes a remarkably competent and comprehensive account of recent trends in scholarship on Jesus in his *Gospel Truth: The New Image of Jesus Emerging from Science and History, and Why It Matters* (New York: Riverhead Books, 1997).

3. Figures are from the World Development Forum, as cited in Diana Eck, *Encountering God: A Spiritual Journey from Bozeman to Banaras*, 202.

4. A couple of leading examples of liberation theology's treatment of Jesus' life, death, and resurrection are Leonardo Boff, *Jesus Christ Liberator* (Maryknoll, N.Y.: Orbis, 1978), and Jon Sobrino, *Christology at the Crossroads* (Maryknoll, N.Y.: Orbis, 1978). Jose Miguez Bonino, ed., compiles several others in his *Faces of Jesus: Latin American Christologies* (Maryknoll, N.Y.: Orbis, 1984).

5. Michael J. Buckley, S.J., *At the Origins of Modern Atheism* (New Haven, Conn.: Yale University Press, 1987).

6. Cited in Diana Eck, *Encountering God*, 202.

7. For a close study of this matter, see Raymond Brown, *Jesus God and Man* (Milwaukee: Bruce, 1967), reprinted as an appendix in his more recent *An Introduction to New Testament Christology* (Mahwah, N.J.: Paulist Press, 1994). Brown holds that there is a third clear instance in Hebrews 1, but the language there seems quite ambiguous.

8. This is more fully explicated in Kathleen Fischer and Thomas Hart, *Christian Foundations*, rev. ed., 47–75.

9. Several books besides those by Hart, Nolan, and Borg mentioned above, in which a reformulation of Jesus' relationship with God based on contemporary scholarship can be found are Piet Schoonenberg, *The Christ* (New York: Herder and Herder, 1971);

Notes

Karl Rahner, *Foundations of Christian Faith* (New York: Crossroad, 1978); Gerard Sloyan, *Jesus in Focus* (Mystic, Conn.: Twenty-Third Publications, 1984); Leonard Swidler, *Yeshua: A Model for Moderns* (Kansas City, Mo.: Sheed and Ward, 1988); and Elizabeth Johnson, *Consider Jesus: Waves of Renewal in Christology* (New York: Crossroad, 1990).

10. The question of Jesus' uniqueness and of Christianity's place among the religions of the world is intelligently discussed in scholarly anthologies such as John Hick and Paul Knitter, eds., *The Myth of Christian Uniqueness* (Maryknoll, N.Y.: Orbis, 1987) and Leonard Swidler, ed., *Toward a Universal Theology of Religion* (Maryknoll, N.Y.: Orbis, 1987). See also Diana Eck, op. cit., 166–99.

11. Some scholars think that Jesus may have identified himself with the expected servant-prophet spoken of in Isaiah 42–53, and so may have seen his coming death as expiation.

12. I treat the question of what salvation means more at length in my *To Know and Follow Jesus*, 7–23. Marcus Borg, in his *Meeting Jesus Again for the First Time* (Harper San Francisco, 1994), 130–37, elaborates a critique of the satisfaction theory.

Chapter 6. Is a Relationship with the Mystery Possible for Me?

1. For a brief summary of these approaches, and suggestions for further reading, see Kathleen Fischer and Thomas Hart, *Christian Foundations*, rev. ed., 13–30.

2. Edith Hamilton, *The Greek Way* (New York: Norton, 1930), 64–65.

3. William James, *Varieties of Religious Experience* (New York: Macmillan, 1961), 393, italics his.

4. Alfred North Whitehead, *Process and Reality* (New York: Macmillan, 1929), 408.

5. Rudolph Otto, *The Idea of the Holy* (Harmondsworth, Middlesex, England: Pelican Books, 1959), 45.

Chapter 7. Toward a Life-Giving Christian Spirituality:
Ten Guiding Principles

1. I describe the interplay between psychology and spirituality in therapy, both theoretically and in case studies, in Thomas Hart, *Hidden Spring: The Spiritual Dimension of Therapy* (Mahwah, N.J.: Paulist Press, 1995).

2. Edward Schillebeeckx, *Jesus: An Experiment in Christology* (New York: Crossroad, 1979), 140–54.

3. For a fine treatment of the problem of evil in the world in the face of God's goodness, see Harold Kushner, *When Bad Things Happen to Good People* (New York: Schocken Books, 1981); William P. Roberts, "God and Prayer When You're Suffering," in *Praying*, no. 19 (July-August 1987): 4; Wendy Farley, *Tragic Vision and Divine Compassion: A Contemporary Theodicy* (Louisville: Westminster John Knox, 1990).

4. See Wilkie Au, *By Way of the Heart* (Mahwah, N.J.: Paulist Press, 1989), 67.

5. For a clear summary of Whitehead's thought on God's creative love as persuasive and as interested in promoting creaturely enjoyment, see John Cobb and David Griffin, *Process Theology* (Philadelphia: Westminster, 1976), 52–57.

6. I elaborate these ideas more fully in my book on spiritual direction, Thomas Hart, *The Art of Christian Listening* (Mahwah, N.J.: Paulist Press, 1980), chapters 7 and 8.

7. See the "Rules for the Discernment of Spirits" in George E. Ganss, S.J., ed., *Ignatius of Loyola: The Spiritual Exercises and Selected Works* Classics of Western Spirituality, vol. 72 (Mahwah, N.J.: Paulist Press, 1991), 201–7.

Chapter 8. Spirituality and Sexuality

1. For a fine development of the idea of sexuality as lively dynamism toward relatedness, see Judith Plaskow, *Standing Again at Sinai: Judaism from a Feminist Perspective* (New York: HarperCollins, 1991), 170–210.

2. Beverly Wildung Harrison portrays this unity compellingly in her "Human Sexuality and Mutuality," Judith L. Weidman, ed., *Christian Feminism: Visions of a New Humanity* (New York: Harper and Row, 1984), 141–57.

3. Some appreciation of this begins finally to shine in the Second Vatican Council's treatment of the married vocation in the 1960s. But the celebration of sexuality itself is quiet and confined to this single context, heterosexual marriage. See chapter 1 of the document "Pastoral Constitution on the Church in the Modern World," in Walter M. Abbott, S.J., *The Documents of Vatican II* (New York: America Press, 1966), 249–58.

4. Some books by Christian pastors and theologians who regard sexuality positively and take an intelligently nuanced approach to its moral norms are Evelyn Eaton Whitehead and James D. Whitehead, *A Sense of Sexuality* (New York: Doubleday, 1989); James B. Nelson, *Embodiment: An Approach to Sexuality and Christian Theology* (Minneapolis: Augsburg, 1978); James B. Nelson, *Between Two Gardens: Reflections on Sexuality and Religious Experience* (Cleveland: Pilgrim Press, 1983); John J. McNeill, *Taking a Chance on God: Liberating Theology for Gays, Lesbians, and Their Lovers, Families, and Friends* (Boston: Beacon Press, 1988); John Shelby Spong, *Living in Sin?: A Bishop Rethinks Human Sexuality* (New York: Harper and Row, 1988). Thomas Fox, in his *Sexuality and Catholicism* (New York: George Braziller, 1995), gives us the history of Roman Catholic thought on sexual issues from ancient times to the present.

Chapter 9. The Movement of the Spirit and the Challenge to the Churches

1. Charles Dickson, "Listening to the Unchurched," in *The Priest*, January 1996.

2. Marcus Borg, *The God We Never Knew*, 70.

3. For an account of the beginnings of the movement and its significance for Latin America, see Leonardo Boff, *Ecclesiogenesis: The Base*

Communities Reinvent the Church (Maryknoll, N.Y.: Orbis, 1986). Bernard Lee and Michael Cowan were among the first to chronicle the movement in the world and in the United States. See their *Dangerous Memories: House Churches and Our American Story* (Kansas City, Mo.: Sheed and Ward, 1986) and their *Conversation, Risk, and Conversion: The Life of Small Christian Communities* (Maryknoll, N.Y.: Orbis, 1997). Some other books on the base community movement are David Janzen et al., *Fire, Salt, and Peace: Intentional Christian Communities Alive in North America* (Evanston, Ill.: Shalom Mission Communities, 1997); Margaret O'Connell Bisgrove, *Where Two Are Gathered: Stories of 12 Small Christian Communities* (Winona, Minn.: St. Mary's Press, 1996); Harrison Burke et al., *People, Promise and Community: A Practical Guide to Creating and Sustaining Small Communities of Faith* (Mahwah, N.J.: Paulist Press, 1997).

4. For some twenty documents which grew out of world-level bilateral ecumenical conversations between 1972–95, see William Rusch and Jeffrey Gros, eds., *Deepening Communion* (Mahwah, N.J.: Paulist Press, 1998).

5. (New York: The Free Press,1996), 5.

6. See, for example, Bernard Lee, *The Future Church of 140 B.C.E.: A Hidden Revolution* (New York: Crossroad, 1995).

7. The Rev. Robert E. Schmitz, "Of Dinosaurs, Carrier Pigeons, and Disappearing Priests," in *America*, 175, 10 (Oct. 12, 1996), 11.